DAN SATER'S
European Classics

TUSCAN, ITALIAN, FRENCH, SPANISH & ENGLISH

Eighty

DESIGNER HOME PLANS

A DESIGNS DIRECT PUBLISHING BOOK

Presented by

The Sater Design Collection, Inc.
The Center at the Springs
25241 Elementary Way, Suite 201, Bonita Springs, FL 34135

Dan F. Sater, II — CEO and Author

Rickard Bailey — Editor-in-Chief

Jennifer Baker — Editor

CONTRIBUTING WRITERS

Laura Hurst Brown, Alan Lopuszynski, Matt McGarry,

Marla Ottenstein, Clare Ulik

Dave Jenkins — Illustrator

Patrick Chin Shue — Production Illustrator

CG Renderer Visualization Studio, Inc. — Virtual Illustrator

Diane Zwack — Creative Director/Art Director

Kim Campeau — Graphic Artist

Emily Sessa — Graphic Artist

CONTRIBUTING PHOTOGRAPHERS

Brynn Bruijn, Tom Harper, Richard Leo Johnson, Joseph Lapeyra,

Michael Lowry, Kim Sargent, Larry Taylor, Doug Thompson,

Oscar Thompson, CJ Walker and Jerry Willis

Front Cover Photos: Joseph Lapeyra, Kim Sargent, CJ Walker
Back Cover Photos: Joseph Lapeyra and CJ Walker
Front Flap Image: Joseph Lapeyra

Printed by: Toppan Printing Co., China

First Printing: September 2007

10 9 8 7 6 5 4 3 2 1

Spanish

French colonial

$\mathscr{C}$ontents

European influences in architecture and style

In creating this series of designs, my intent was not to replicate European designs, but rather to capture the essence of the classic beauty inherent in each archetype. Classical Old-World architecture significantly influenced early American residential design in several ways. Admirers of great masters, such as Thomas Jefferson, brought back these ideas and design elements and eagerly sought to incorporate them into a truly American style. It is with this same passion that we bring you "European Classics," a New-World portfolio of distinctly American homes—representing not replicas but new designs that borrow from the character and magic of these masterpieces. We have integrated history-rich exteriors with plans that include all of the state-of-the-art conveniences and amenities one would expect in a modern American home.

For this collection, I selected five regions of European influence: Italian, Tuscan, French, English and Spanish. Each of these archetypes have played an important role in the development of American residential design.

I hope you will find in these home plans a sense of heritage, not only in timeless exterior elevations, but also in well-planned interiors that incorporate thoughtful intimate spaces with ultra-functional modern amenities.

May God grant his blessings of peace, prosperity and joy to your home and all who reside within!

Dan F. Sater II, AIBD, CPBD

T uscan architecture is a pre-classical Italianate style of rustic villas and farmhouses that evolved from readily available materials found in the Tuscan hillside and fields: such as fieldstone, rough-hewn wood and terracotta clay. Paramount to the design is the rapport between the interior and exterior living areas, as manifest in the prevalence of open courtyards, walkways and loggias. Warm, vibrant "earth-toned" colors, evocative of the sun-kissed hillside, are characteristic of a Tuscan-themed home, as is the use of textured wall finishes, rough-hewn wooden flooring, natural stone tiles and rustic beamed ceilings.

Decorative elements, such as stone columns, arches and cornices, as well as terracotta roofs, cobblestone walkways, richly painted stucco façades and wrought-iron accents, play an important roll in creating the comfortable, Old-World ambiance that is associated with Tuscan design.

N o country has more profoundly influenced residential architecture than Italy. Great masters such as Vignola, Palladio and Bernini employed great skill in practicing their craft. No one, however, impacted residential design like Palladio, who understood the importance of the relationship between the home and its site.

Classical architects also understood the relationship of the home to its occupants. In fact, classical architecture may be construed as an embodiment of the human form, seeking to relate building proportions to human scale. The Italians developed a mastery of these techniques, and in addition gave us a mix of grand porticos and turrets, trefoil windows, cut-stone masonry, carved eave brackets and spiral columns.

American styles that reflect direct Italian influences are Renaissance, Tuscan and Baroque.

French | 8017

REVIVAL

LES TOURELLES

French architecture extended the concepts of scale and site relative to houses with a heightened sense of grandeur and luxe detail. Residential design reached its greatest heights under the tutelage of French kings who, impressed by Italian life and art, sought to emulate the rich aesthetics and translate them into a French style. Great French architects such as Philibert de l'Orame and Jacques Androuet du Cereceau, and later François Mansart, defined this style by focusing on the use of ornament over form. French kings and the "nouveau riche" built many grand mansions, incorporating art as architecture and adding new features such as porte-cocheres, galleries and grand staircases. The use of steeply pitched roofs punctuated with ornamented dormers, flared eaves, rusticated pilasters and quoins became common elements in crowning French homes. The use of columns divorced from arches was also a departure from the Roman influence, and became an important part of French classical architecture.

American styles that reflect French influences are Chateauesque, Beaux Arts, French Provincial (Country) and Second Empire.

English | 8008

RURAL

NEW ABBEY

England was also greatly influenced by Italian design aesthetics, as well as French architecture. Yet British architects such as Inigo Jones and his contemporaries developed their own unique style by implementing Palladian concepts with a decidedly British flair. Rugged exterior textures, stately gables and pediments, keystone arches and plentiful multi-pane windows created welcoming façades reminiscent of the English countryside.

Aside from the obvious, it is easy to understand the direct English influence on American architecture. With transcontinental waves of immigrants came a wealth of variants on the dominant British styles. Benjamin Latrobe, the first professional architect to practice in America, was born in Yorkshire and trained in London. He drew plans for the White House and other notable public buildings, and later influenced a generation of leading American designers.

American styles influenced by the British Isles are Georgian, Colonial Revival, Gothic (Tudor), Victorian and Classical Revival, to name a few.

Spanish | 8052

VILLA-STYLE

CAPRINA

Spanish architecture was influenced not only by elements of Italian and French design, but by Moorish styles as well. Coupled with Native American building techniques, the eclectic dialects of the Spanish vernacular led to a truly unique archetype in home design. Elaborate entry turrets, quatrefoil windows, low-pitched rooflines, carved balustrades and rounded arches became a few of the style's defining traits.

Andalusian and Moorish influences altered the home's relationship with nature, with such residential features as courtyards, interior fountains and arched loggias. The use of brightly colored tile mosaics for decoration on sculpted stucco and stone facades extended the Spanish vernacular and is practiced with artful skill in modern revivals.

American styles that reflect Spanish influences are Mediterranean, Spanish Colonial and Monterey.

Italian | CUSTOM

VILLA-STYLE

MONTEVERDI

FOR SIMILAR DESIGN SEE PAGE 132

FRONT EXTERIOR

With its multiple-hip roofline, intricately fashioned cast-stone detailing and copious arched windows and entryways, the Monteverdi typifies the quintessential Northern Italian estate home. A pair of wrought-iron gates draws the eye toward the magnificent arched entryway, which is flanked on either side by two balustrade-enhanced terraces.

FOYER/WET BAR

A profusion of natural sunlight enters the foyer through a wrought-iron sheathed transom, accentuating the stone art niche. Adjacent to the foyer, the centerpiece of the wet bar area is the gorgeously painted and hand-stenciled groin ceiling.

PHOTOGRAPHY: JOSEPH LAPEYRA

KITCHEN

While the octagonal-shaped, beamed and coffered ceiling draws the eye upward, a dramatically sloped, stone-and-tile hood acts to balance the room's height. Stunningly veined granite countertops, including a cleverly split center island, complement the room's custom milled cabinetry.

REAR DECK VIEW

When designing this home, the goal was to embrace the spectacular views and incorporate them into the overall design. The outdoor fireplace, with its faultless detailing and two-way hearth, strengthens the relationship between the adjacent family room and outdoor living room by bringing the two rooms together as one.

FAMILY ROOM

The family room opens onto the covered loggia through an expansive wall of retreating glass doors. The natural transition between the indoor living spaces and the outdoors is paramount to the intrinsic design and flow of the home.

LIVING ROOM

The fireplace, with its elaborate cut-stone surround, is flanked on either side by a pair of deep-set display niches. Just like a beautifully framed painting, the three-panel window draws attention to views of the stunning pool area.

MASTER BEDROOM

A succession of decorative columns seemingly supports the triple-stepped coffered ceiling, creating an intimate, canopy-like setting. Above the bed, a corbel-enhanced, arched niche blends into a tier of crown moulding creating a memorable milieu.

MASTER BATH

A glass window separates the tub from the spacious walk-thru shower, which is accessible on either side through a pair of arched openings. Astute detailing, including the arched and mirrored vanity and several beautifully tiled surfaces, further enhance the master bath.

STUDY

The centerpiece of the study is the magnificently carved marble fireplace. The façade, a fusion of linear influences and organically themed carvings, is one of the home's many focal points. Mullioned windows with corresponding arched transoms invite the outdoors inside.

French | CUSTOM
COLONIAL
SANABRIA

FOR SIMILAR DESIGN SEE PAGE 155

FRONT EXTERIOR

Wide porches and hipped roofs—freely adapted from Colonial Revival styles—collaborate with triple dormers and decorative shutters in creating a simply stunning façade.

ENTRY FOYER

The parlor creates an intimate, fluid boundary between the entry porch and the rear veranda. An elegant yet comfortable theme prevails throughout the home, with immediate transitions to outside living areas from the public rooms. A gallery connecting the stair hall with the great room and kitchen sports a niche with a built-in glass cabinet.

REAR DECK/ POOL

A balcony accessed from the upstairs guest suites follows the extended perimeter of the home and offers wide-open views. Multiple sets of glass doors integrate the interior and outdoor living spaces into one.

REAR VIEW

An enchanting blend of seaside finesse and colonial charm, this waterfront home extends towards the harbor in graduating levels from the rear veranda. The pool and spa area leads up to an alfresco dining space as well as down to the dock.

GREAT ROOM

Comfortable and elegant, the great room opens on both sides to the veranda and solana via sets of retractable French doors, providing a free flow of traffic to the sitting area, fireplace and outdoor kitchen.

OFFICE/STUDY

Exposed trusses iterate the symmetry and informality of the plan in the study. Tall windows and transoms frame a pair of opposing French doors that open to a balcony and upper lanai. Paneled doors flanking the entertainment center lead to hall storage and a bonus guest suite.

MASTER BEDROOM

The spacious master suite enjoys panoramic views through the bay windows found in the sitting nook. Fresh air streams in from French doors connecting the room to the loggia.

Italian CUSTOM

VILLA-STYLE

RAFINA

FOR SIMILAR DESIGN SEE PAGE 26

© THE SATER DESIGN COLLECTION, INC.

FRONT VIEW

An elaborate recessed entry lined with decorative brackets sets off a hipped roof and cupola, which provide the definitive elements to the plan's Italianate roots. The rusticated surround enriches authentic details such as carved corbels and corner quoins, and repeats the arched forms of the colonnade.

DINING ROOM

Entertaining around a carved anigre dining table is made elegantly simple with a nearby butler's pantry and the kitchen just beyond. Deep-red velvet drapes outline the artful views of an elegant covered deck framed by strong tapered columns.

GRAND SALON

A masterpiece of simplicity, the glass-walled grand salon exhibits open, unrestrained space anchored by a two-story fireplace and breathtaking views. Beyond a trio of radius windows and French doors, glimpses of the fountain, pool and spa bring in a sense of nature. A deeply carved cherry mantel captures the focus of the room.

KITCHEN

Exposed timber beams and a tongue-and-groove cypress ceiling animate the rustic qualities of the high-tech kitchen. The mosaic tile backsplash echoes the pattern of a decorative platter above the cook-top. Beyond the food-prep area is a butler's pantry, which leads to the dining room.

REAR DECK

High arches wrap the screen-enclosed pool-and-spa area, visually uniting the outer zone with the rear elevation. The loggia harbors flexible sitting areas, while the upper porch belongs to a game room designed for both family and friends.

MASTER BATH

Elegant columns sentinel a large bow window overlooking a carefully organized landscape. Sable-colored marble surrounds the spa-style tub, and candlelight mimics the glow of a vintage gilt chandelier.

MASTER BEDROOM

Amber-glazed walls create an envelope of calm in the owner's retreat, which includes a sitting bay with views of the rear property. Floor-to-ceiling damask drapes soften the tall windows that surround the cozy sitting area.

POOL/FOUNTAIN

With the rear sited toward a lake and lush fairways, the plan takes on an attitude of relaxed luxury, and maintains an informal spirit.

Spanish CUSTOM
COURTYARD
VILLORESI

SIDE VIEW

Hispanic elements, such as the multi-level roof and double-sash doors, lend eclectic qualities to the façade of this courtyard villa. Roman Doric columns, carved balustrades and sculpted arches line the paired balconies.

FRONT ENTRY

This plan employs a shapely balustrade to animate the façade and visually connect the formal entry to the street-level porte-cochere. With turn-of-the-century grandeur, the staircase exhibits the carefree nature of a home by the sea with a playful sweeping curve.

GALLERY

Lava-grey and bianco stone tiles create a classic checkerboard pattern on the floor of the gallery. Imagined as an exhibit hall for the owner's valuable art collection, the passage permits plenty of natural light to illuminate the displays. The ultra-linear dimensions of the space are transformed by sets of glass doors leading out to the courtyard.

COURTYARD

Crisp, rectilinear lines frame the splendid courtyard placed at the center of the home's lateral wings. Roman Doric columns and sculpted arches border the rear perimeter. To the left of the upper portico, top gables recede from the roofline, adding a layered texture to the elevation.

DINING ROOM

Rows of glass doors open the formal dining room to the wide courtyard and more intimate loggia. Views pour in through a series of radius windows that line this space and the gallery leading back to the foyer. A coffered ceiling adds depth to the airy dimensions of the room.

GRAND SALON

Infused with sunlight, the grand salon overlooks a large wetlands preserve and opens to a balcony. To the left, a second series of glass doors brings in more light and leads out to the courtyard. Twin archways framing the rear wall offer links to a secluded clubroom.

KITCHEN

Connected to a generous butler's pantry, the gourmet-caliber kitchen is an entertainer's dream. A center island provides dual sinks for easy meal preparation, and built-in cabinetry flanks the convenient eating bar. Nearby, a bay-shaped breakfast nook enjoys panoramic views.

Spanish | 6953
VILLA-STYLE
CORDILLERA

DINING ROOM

Tailored, classic furnishings lend a formal air to the dining room, which leads outdoors to the lanai.

A desire to create a home that paid homage to Palm Beach's great Addison-influenced villas, while at the same time embracing contemporary design ideas and technologies, was the inspiration behind Dan Sater's award-winning *Cordillera*. The recipient of numerous industry awards, this home incorporates modern amenities and elements such as cornerless disappearing sliding-glass walls, clubrooms, outdoor living spaces and full-house automation.

The villa-style plan opens traditionally boxed spaces to satisfying views of the landscape. The vaulted foyer opens through the front gallery to the formal core of the home: a series of three view-oriented rooms designed to encourage intimate gatherings. To the right of the home, the casual living zone incorporates a spacious leisure room that links with a nook and kitchen. Upstairs, a balcony bridge connects a game room, pub and home theater with two guest suites.

FOYER

Corinthian columns and simple Tuscan pilasters line a long colonnade leading the eye toward a terminal vestibule—anchored by a paneled wet bar—which links the casual living area and service hall.

LIVING ROOM

Double-paneled entry doors mirror the symmetry of the intricately carved fireplace and stone surround at the formal center of the home. A second-level balcony, with custom wrought-iron detailing, overlooks the area.

LIVING ROOM

A masterpiece of symmetry, the glass-walled living room exhibits open, but restrained space anchored by a two-story fireplace and breathtaking views.

DINING ROOM

Connected to the living room at the center of the plan, the dining room takes in views of the lanai and lakefront. A stunning stepped ceiling adds a touch of drama to its formality.

NOOK

A stepped ceiling with rustic wood beams and an art niche add a handcrafted touch to the breakfast nook.

SOLANA

The outdoor retreat wraps the leisure room, nook and kitchen with a perfect space for entertaining. Interior and exterior living areas mix seamlessly via retreating glass doors.

KITCHEN

Multiple workstations and state-of-the-art appliances combine with a beamed ceiling and granite countertops to create an inviting and functional kitchen.

LEISURE ROOM

Retreating glass doors provide an intimate connection from the leisure room to the solana, lanai and courtyard. High-end electronics integrated into the design provide surrond-sound, advanced security systems and soft, subtle lighting.

MASTER BEDROOM

Floor-to-ceiling windows permit natural light to permeate the master bedroom. Curved moldings, a coffered ceiling and a flattened arch lend dimension, depth and texture to the room, which leads outside to the lanai, pool and spa.

MASTER BATH

Framed by twin Tuscan columns, a sculpted
Persian-red marble tub surround enhances
the grand scale of the master bath. Past
the tall muntin window and fanlight is a
glimpse of the private garden.

REAR DECK VIEW

Exquisite details enrich the central hip roof that dominates the rear perimeter of the home: an arcature caps the rusticated surround and massive pilasters frame the archway in complementary styles. A row of French doors opens the interior to the outside living area, which overlooks the sun terrace and pool. To the left, the solana dissolves the boundaries of outer and inner spaces and features a fireplace and alfresco kitchen.

MEDIA ROOM

The ultimate entertainment room—a wet bar, home theater and French doors opening to a private deck round out the media room's many amenities.

LEVEL ONE

REAR DECK

Shapely columns and arches create a fluid boundary between the pool deck and solana, and shelter the outside living area from the midday sun.

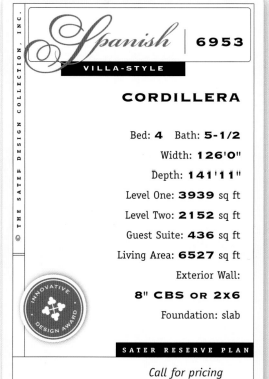

Spanish | 6953

VILLA-STYLE

CORDILLERA

Bed: **4** Bath: **5-1/2**

Width: **126'0"**

Depth: **141'11"**

Level One: **3939** sq ft

Level Two: **2152** sq ft

Guest Suite: **436** sq ft

Living Area: **6527** sq ft

Exterior Wall:

8" CBS OR 2X6

Foundation: slab

INNOVATIVE DESIGN AWARD

SATER RESERVE PLAN

Call for pricing

LEVEL TWO

Spanish | 6932

MOORISH

MARTINIQUE

POWDER BATH

Located near the formal living spaces, the eclectic powder room is enhanced with a stunning wallpaper treatment and dramatic hand-painted cabinetry.

Clearly Mediterranean-inspired, with a barrel-tile roof in terracotta hues, lancet arches and Tuscan columns, the sun-drenched façade of this home extends a formal welcome. Crisp, white trim speaks of Spanish influence, and iron detailing adds a hint of non-conformity.

Past the foyer, an open floor plan emphasizes outdoor living with a seamless transition of indoor and outdoor spaces. Columns, built-ins and ceiling treatments define rooms, while a flowing floor plan creates natural movement.

The formal living room is punctuated by natural light welcomed in by floor-to-ceiling windows. The openness of the leisure room, nook and kitchen create casual gathering areas extended by ample outdoor spaces. Spacious guest accommodations on both floors assure that visitors stay in comfort. Guests enjoy private or semi-private full baths and quiet spaces—a garden on the first floor and a loft upstairs.

DINING ROOM

Directly past the foyer, guests will enjoy an elegant dining experience in the formal dining room. Light pours in through multi-paned windows and transoms, while repeating arches and Corinthian columns enhance the aesthetic appeal of the room.

LIVING ROOM

Elegant arches and stunning wood columns define the dining space, while giving it a unique connection to the diamond-shaped living room. More wood adds drama to a stepped ceiling, and three dramatic windows provide natural light and an effortless connection to the veranda.

LEISURE ROOM

The handcrafted built-in entertainment center and molded ceiling details provide drama to the spacious leisure room, which opens naturally onto the veranda's outdoor kitchen and main entertainment space.

KITCHEN

Well-appointed and well-planned, this kitchen boasts ample storage for tools of the trade and two large islands that add lots of workspace. Ornate woodwork on the cabinetry and soffits adds an exotic flair to this ultra-functional room.

REAR DECK

The veranda features twelve-foot ceilings and wraps along the entire back of the house and around the pool for first-class outdoor living and entertaining.

MASTER BATH

A whirlpool tub in the master bath is anything but ordinary, nestled between dark wood columns and overlooking a private garden.

MASTER BEDROOM

A stepped ceiling with molding details and elegant lighting crowns a generous master suite. An art niche separates two walk-in closets and provides a visually appealing entry to a fully appointed master bedroom.

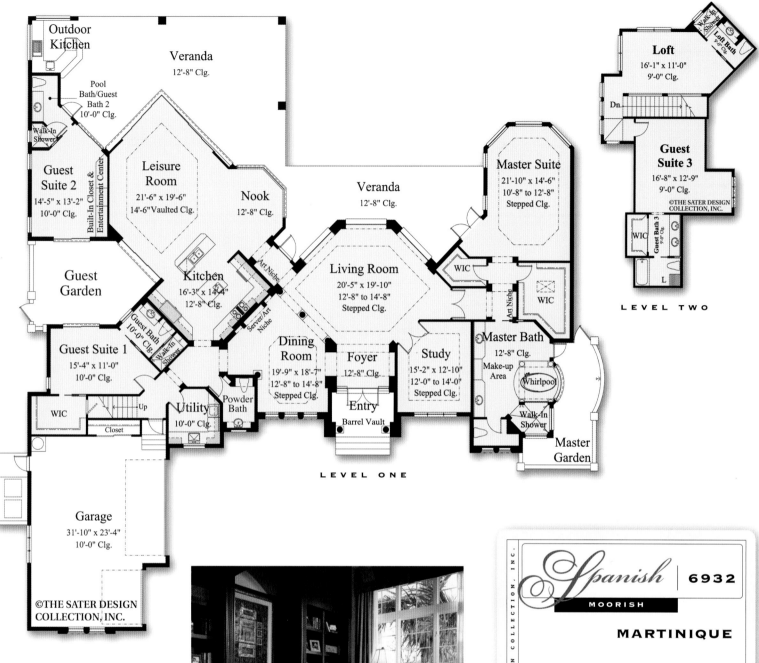

Level Two

Loft
16'-1" x 11'-0"
9'-0" Clg.

Guest Suite 3
16'-8" x 12'-9"
9'-0" Clg.
©THE SATER DESIGN COLLECTION, INC.

Level One

Outdoor Kitchen

Veranda
12'-8" Clg.

Pool Bath/Guest Bath 2
10'-0" Clg.

Guest Suite 2
14'-5" x 13'-2"
10'-0" Clg.

Leisure Room
21'-6" x 19'-6"
14'-6" Vaulted Clg.

Nook
12'-8" Clg.

Veranda
12'-8" Clg.

Master Suite
21'-10" x 14'-6"
10'-8" to 12'-8"
Stepped Clg.

Guest Garden

Kitchen
16'-3" x 14'-4"
12'-8" Clg.

Living Room
20'-5" x 19'-10"
12'-8" to 14'-8"
Stepped Clg.

Guest Suite 1
15'-4" x 11'-0"
10'-0" Clg.

Dining Room
19'-9" x 18'-7"
12'-8" to 14'-8"
Stepped Clg.

Foyer
12'-8" Clg.

Study
15'-2" x 12'-10"
12'-0" to 14'-0"
Stepped Clg.

Master Bath
12'-8" Clg.

Make-up Area

Whirlpool

Utility
10'-0" Clg.

Powder Bath

Entry
Barrel Vault

Walk-In Shower

Master Garden

Garage
31'-10" x 23'-4"
10'-0" Clg.

©THE SATER DESIGN COLLECTION, INC.

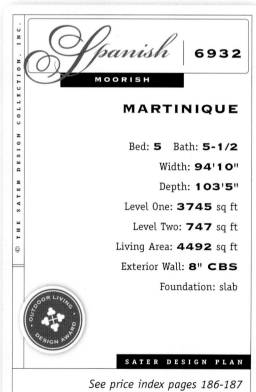

STUDY

This extra-large study has it all: a wall of custom cabinetry, another of windows overlooking a front garden, a stepped ceiling and lots of floor space for working and relaxing.

Spanish | 6932
MOORISH

MARTINIQUE

Bed: **5** Bath: **5-1/2**
Width: **94'10"**
Depth: **103'5"**
Level One: **3745** sq ft
Level Two: **747** sq ft
Living Area: **4492** sq ft
Exterior Wall: **8" CBS**
Foundation: slab

SATER DESIGN PLAN

See price index pages 186-187

English | **6927**

BRITISH COLONIAL

ANDROS ISLAND

From hues and architectural lines that mimic the natural landscape to disappearing walls and a spectacular courtyard that has an indoor feel, the intent of this home is to embrace the outdoors. The dining room, guest suite and study at the front of the home accomplish this with floor-to-ceiling bay windows. In the living room, retreating glass walls create flawless indoor-outdoor transitions. The kitchen flows into a leisure room that also has disappearing sliders to the lanai and courtyard.

Custom details, including a corner entertainment unit in the leisure room and sunburst-laden transoms above the kitchen bar, infuse the home with individuality. The master suite reveals elegant respite starting with the entry foyer and continuing into a walk-in shower that merges with a private outdoor garden. The second-level bonus room offers a substantial flexible space that includes a full bathroom and balcony.

PHOTOGRAPHY: LARRY TAYLOR

DINING ROOM

An octagonal tray ceiling and bay windows illuminate the expansive space of the dining room and lend sophistication to every meal. A built-in buffet fits elegantly into a lighted wall niche that's perfect for a treasured piece of artwork.

LIVING ROOM

Zero-corner glass walls disappear to expand the living room onto the lanai. The layered molding adds flair, and the room's unique shape is a creative setting for flexible seating.

COURTYARD

The possibilities for entertaining are endless in this captivating courtyard adjacent to the lanai. Columns, tray ceilings and tile floors exude an indoor feel, while the island-inspired fireplace, kitchen and hearty furniture embrace any climactic changes.

KITCHEN

The lateral arrangement between the leisure room and kitchen, with nearby breakfast nook, creates a casual zone that is a great place for relaxing with friends and snacks.

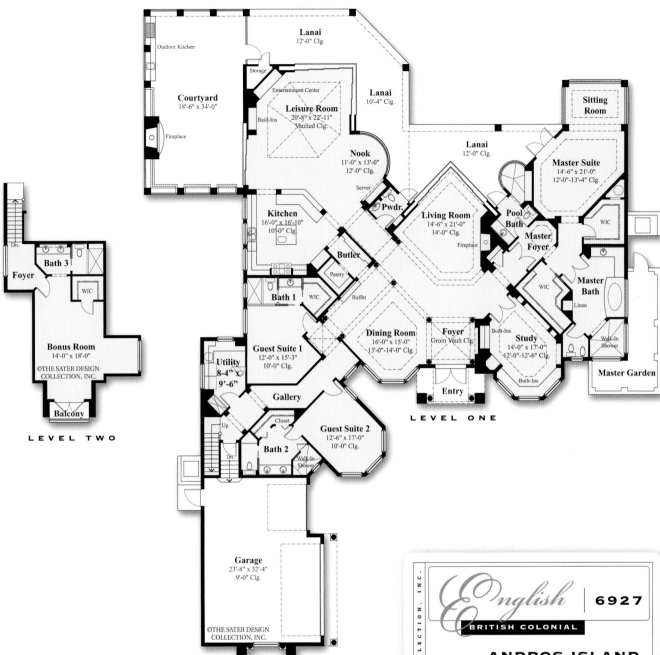

LEVEL TWO

Foyer

Bath 3

WIC

Bonus Room
14'-0" x 18'-0"

©THE SATER DESIGN
COLLECTION, INC.

Balcony

Dn.

Courtyard
18'-6" x 34'-0"

Outdoor Kitchen

Fireplace

Lanai
12'-0" Clg.

Storage

Entertainment Center

Built-Ins

Leisure Room
20'-8" x 22'-11"
Vaulted Clg.

Lanai
10'-4" Clg.

Nook
11'-0" x 13'-0"
12'-0" Clg.

Server

Kitchen
16'-0" x 16'-10"
10'-0" Clg.

Butler

Pantry

Pwdr.

Living Room
14'-6" x 21'-0"
14'-0" Clg.

Fireplace

Lanai
12'-0" Clg.

Sitting Room

Master Suite
14'-6" x 21'-0"
12'-0"-13'-4" Clg.

WIC

Pool Bath

Master Foyer

WIC

Master Bath

Linen

Bath 1

WIC

Buffet

Guest Suite 1
12'-0" x 15'-3"
10'-0" Clg.

Dining Room
16'-0" x 15'-0"
13'-0"-14'-0" Clg.

Foyer
Groin Vault Clg.

Built-Ins

Study
14'-0" x 17'-0"
12'-0"-12'-6" Clg.

Built-Ins

Walk-In Shower

Master Garden

Utility
8'-4" x 9'-6"

Gallery

Entry

LEVEL ONE

Closet

Up

Guest Suite 2
12'-6" x 17'-0"
10'-0" Clg.

Bath 2

Walk-In Shower

Dn.

Garage
23'-8" x 32'-4"
9'-0" Clg.

©THE SATER DESIGN
COLLECTION, INC.

A meandering lanai follows the unusual lines of the back of the home, where a circular glass-walled breakfast nook and disappearing glass walls in the living room blur the lines between indoors and out.

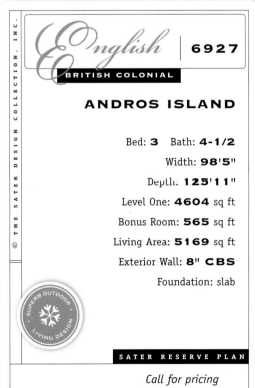

English | **6927**
BRITISH COLONIAL

ANDROS ISLAND

Bed: **3**   Bath: **4-1/2**

Width: **98'5"**

Depth: **125'11"**

Level One: **4604** sq ft

Bonus Room: **565** sq ft

Living Area: **5169** sq ft

Exterior Wall: **8" CBS**

Foundation: slab

SUPERB OUTDOOR LIVING DESIGN

SATER RESERVE PLAN

Call for pricing

© THE SATER DESIGN COLLECTION, INC.

Italian | **6954**

MEDITERRANEAN

DI MORA

Corbelled cornices, decorative-quoin elements and keystone-enhanced arches, coupled with a capriciously gabled roofline, reinforce the home's Italian-inspired design. The true essence of the home is the amalgamation of interior and exterior spaces, thus maximizing the functionality of the home. While myriad windows and glass doors strengthen the constant connection between the inside and outdoors, the study, dining and living rooms transition freely into one another.

To the left of the foyer, the wet bar differentiates the informal and formal venues. In the kitchen and family room, retreating glass doors open onto the covered lanai and pool deck, creating a "room without walls." To the right of the foyer, the master suite, with its large sitting alcove, oversized walk-in closet and luxuriously appointed bath and private courtyard, is a serene milieu that is unsurpassed.

WET BAR

With its generously curved, two-tiered granite countertop and stone-enhanced art niche, the wet bar serves as an anchor, joining the casual family room and kitchen to the formal living and dining areas.

PHOTOGRAPHY: MICHAEL LOWRY

DINING ROOM

The detailed, triple-tiered ceiling envelops the magnificent dining room. From the large art niche to the glass-fronted French doors, every detail comes together as one, creating a picture-perfect design.

LEISURE ROOM

Retreating glass doors seemingly pull the outdoors inside toward the leisure room, kitchen and nook, creating a large, wide-open living space. Enhanced by custom millwork elements, the family room's exaggerated sloped-tray ceiling creates a cozy ambiance.

KITCHEN

The kitchen, with its octagonal-shaped, beamed coffered ceiling and center prep island, opens up into the family room and nook. The angled breakfast bar and arched side entries define the exclusivity of the separate spaces, while at the same time joining them as one.

MASTER BEDROOM

Through a row of windows in the bay-shaped sitting alcove, as well as through a pair of adjacent French doors, a profusion of sunlight infuses the luxuriously detailed master suite. The double-tiered coffered ceiling adds depth and interest, resulting in a peaceful owners' retreat.

MASTER BATH

Set back into an arched niche, a large mirror captures reflections of the adjoining private garden. In the center of the room, the tile surround and deck of the oval-shaped tub incorporates the same intricate detailing as in the stunning walk-in shower.

STUDY

Custom-designed, floor-to-ceiling built-ins enhance the study's distinctly understated, yet masculine character. Bordering the master suite, the focal point of the room is the triple-tiered, octagonal-shaped ceiling, into which a dropped soffit detail has been skillfully introduced.

REAR VIEW

The verandah, with its corresponding columns and broadly arched openings, spans from one side of the home to the other, strengthening the transition and connectivity of the indoors to the outdoors through copious window walls and entryways.

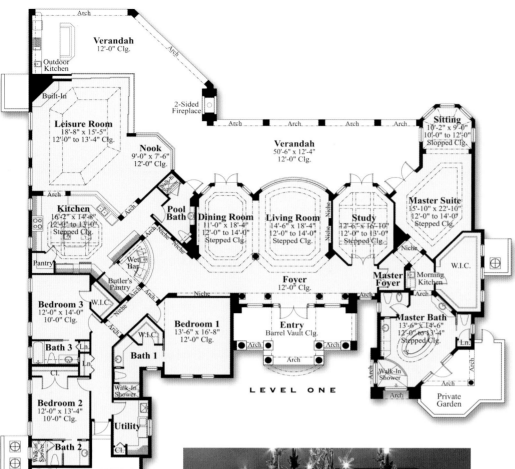

LEVEL ONE

Verandah
12'-0" Clg.

Outdoor
Kitchen

Built-In

Leisure Room
18'-8" x 15'-5"
12'-0" to 13'-4" Clg.

Nook
9'-0" x 7'-6"
12'-0" Clg.

2-Sided
Fireplace

Arch

Verandah
50'-6" x 12'-4"
12'-0" Clg.

Sitting
10'-2" x 9'-0"
10'-0" to 12'-0"
Sloped Clg.

Kitchen
16'-2" x 14'-8"
12'-0" to 13'-0"
Stepped Clg.

Pool
Bath

Dining Room
11'-0" x 18'-4"
12'-0" to 14'-0"
Stepped Clg.

Living Room
14'-6" x 18'-4"
12'-0" Clg.
Stepped Clg.

Study
12'-6" x 16'-10"
12'-0" to 13'-0"
Stepped Clg.

Master Suite
15'-10" x 22'-10"
12'-0" to 14'-0"
Stepped Clg.

Wet
Bar

Pantry

Butler's
Pantry

W.I.C.

Morning
Kitchen

W.I.C.

Bedroom 3
12'-0" x 14'-0"
10'-0" Clg.

W.I.C.

Foyer
12'-0" Clg.

Master
Foyer

Bath 3

Niche

Bedroom 1
13'-6" x 16'-8"
12'-0" Clg.

Entry
Barrel Vault Clg.

Master Bath
13'-6" x 14'-6"
12'-0" to 13'-0"
Stepped Clg.

Bath 1

W.I.C.

Walk-In
Shower

Walk-In
Shower

Private
Garden

Bedroom 2
12'-0" x 13'-4"
10'-0" Clg.

Utility

Bath 2

Walk-In
Shower

3-Car Garage
22'-4" x 32'-0"
10'-0" Clg.

©THE SATER DESIGN
COLLECTION, INC.

Located across from the butler's pantry, a convenient bedroom features a full bath and includes the luxury of a walk-in closet.

LIVING ROOM

An enormous, three-panel mitered window accentuates the curvature of the room, drawing the eye toward the pool's spectacularly conceived water feature. The highly crowned, triple-tiered ceiling mimics the shape of the room, strengthening the rapport between the interior and exterior elements.

© THE SATER DESIGN COLLECTION, INC.

Italian | **6954**

MEDITERRANEAN

DI MORA

Bed: **4**   Bath: **5**

Width: **94'2"**

Depth: **131'6"**

Level One: **4664** sq ft

Living Area: **4664** sq ft

Exterior Wall: **8" CBS**

Foundation: slab

ELEGANT LIVING DESIGN

SATER DESIGN PLAN

See price index pages 186-187

Italian | 8055
VILLA-STYLE
SAN FILIPPO

Fromm the old-country styling of the central turret to the high ceilings and gracefully arched doorways and windows, *San Filippo* melds award-winning design with comfortable living. Experience breathtaking vistas immediately upon entering the foyer, where an open floor plan allows views directly into the formal dining and living rooms and out through multiple French doors to the veranda.

Nearby, the open kitchen also affords unobstructed views of the nook and leisure room. Retreating glass doors expand the common living space to the outdoor living areas. Upstairs, French doors open two of the four guest bedrooms onto a private deck overlooking the veranda. Enjoying privacy away from the rest of the home, *San Filippo's* master suite must be seen to be believed. The homeowner will relish the massive bedroom, gorgeously stepped ceiling, veranda access and opulent master bath.

FRONT DETAIL

San Filippo welcomes with a deep portico entry and striking turret design. Through a triple archway entrance, three sets of glass doors with arched transoms reveal the foyer and formal living room.

LIVING ROOM

The grand, two-story barrel-vault ceiling is sure to impress, but the careful attention to detail will not go unnoticed. From the transom-topped glass doors leading to the veranda—to the elegant art niches that flank the soaring fireplace—this living room can be the centerpiece of both family gatherings and large-scale entertaining.

DINING ROOM

The loft balcony creates an elegant over-look to the open living room below, while at the same time creating a dining room area with a lower ceiling for cozy, inti-mate meals. The multiple French doors with high-arching transoms open the house to an impressive outdoor living space.

KITCHEN/NOOK

This wide-open common living area is where the nook, kitchen and generous leisure room meet, surrounding a wraparound eating bar of elegant detail and style.

WET BAR

The wet bar is one of several modifications that the homeowner's inserted in the design. The arched doorways connect multiple open areas nearby, including a butler's pantry and dining nook.

MASTER BATH

Designed to be an indulgent retreat, the master bath offers repose with a whirlpool tub and a generous walk-thru shower framed by a triple set of circular windows and repeating arches.

MASTER BEDROOM

The master suite is the very picture of quiet, private grace, featuring a stepped ceiling and a striking bay window overlooking the pool.

REAR VIEW

Allowing boisterous and fun outdoor gatherings to quite late-night contemplations, the indoor and outdoor living spaces provides many different opportunities for family and friends.

VERANDA

Retreating glass doors open the kitchen, nook and leisure room to the veranda where multiple outdoor living areas are found, including a fireplace with built-in entertainment center.

MEDIA ROOM

On the upper level, a guest bedroom was converted into a state-of-the-art media room. Custom built-ins and a spectacular home theater create a gathering place like no other for friends and family.

KITCHEN

A perfect combination of function and style, the kitchen includes a stepped ceiling, convenient pantry and work island with prep sink. It's also a very open area affording easy access to a nearby nook and leisure room.

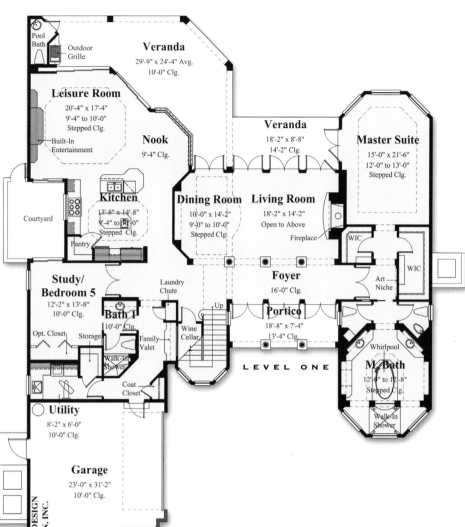

LEVEL ONE

LEVEL TWO

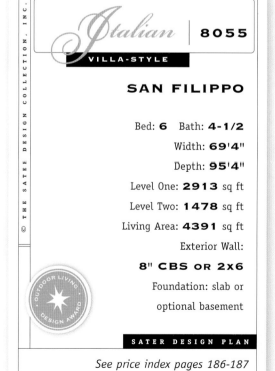

Italian | 8055

VILLA-STYLE

SAN FILIPPO

Bed: **6**   Bath: **4-1/2**

Width: **69'4"**

Depth: **95'4"**

Level One: **2913** sq ft

Level Two: **1478** sq ft

Living Area: **4391** sq ft

Exterior Wall:

8" CBS OR 2X6

Foundation: slab or optional basement

SATER DESIGN PLAN

See price index pages 186-187

Italian | 8046
COURTYARD
LA REINA

njoy the very best that outdoor living has to offer with *La Reina*, a stunning courtyard plan in which classic European beauty meets modern convenience and style. This design features living spaces that flow freely from one room to the next and open doors and balconies to the outside at multiple points throughout.

And while the sensational portico, guest suite and courtyard area are sure to become favorite gathering areas for family and friends, you'll find the charm and beauty within *La Reina's* main house virtually unmatched. The luxuriant and private master suite abounds in open space and refined details. The gourmet kitchen affords quick, open access to the nook, leisure room and dining room—all of which feature magnificent views of the outdoors. And the three additional bedrooms on the upper level offer quiet seclusion, with access to private balconies.

ENTRY FOUNTAIN

Past the doors of the groin-vaulted portico, an expansive courtyard includes two loggias, an outdoor kitchen, fireplace, pool and a detached guest suite that flexes as a private retreat or home office.

GRAND ROOM

Soaring two-story ceilings allow for voluminous views and light to stream in through numerous windows that encircle the room. A grand fireplace provides a central gathering area, and a flowing design offers an open avenue to the dining room nearby.

KITCHEN

Centrally located between the formal and informal rooms, the gourmet-caliber kitchen serves both realms with ease. A wraparound eating bar offers "patrons" a place to sit, while the center island with prep sink provides ample counter space for the family "chef."

NOOK

Light streams in to the bayed breakfast nook through multi-pane windows. A built-in window seat offers storage and a cozy place to sit. Past the archway, the open foyer leads to the grand room.

COURTYARD

Not only visually stunning, the courtyard is a zen-like retreat for family and friends to relax and unwind. A mix of retreating glass and French doors in the master retreat, dining room, detached guest suite and leisure room integrate the interior with the expansive outdoor living area.

MASTER BEDROOM

Designed for privacy and appointed in elegance, the master suite features a high stepped ceiling and generous views through the suite's multi-pane windows and transoms. French doors provide private access to the loggia.

MASTER BATH

This master bath opens to the impressive courtyard area and features a whirlpool tub soaked in light from the outdoors, a beautifully stepped ceiling and arches setting off the suite's vanities.

SIDE VIEW

From the carved balusters to the decorative tile vents and arched window "trios" that circumscribe the house, **La Reina** *features design details around every corner.*

View above shows altered one-car garage, not available in plan.

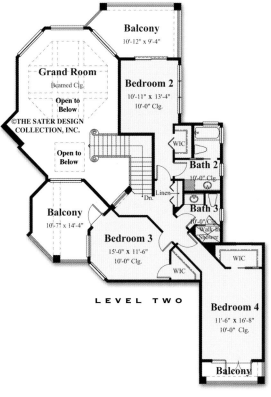

LEVEL TWO

LEVEL ONE

Italian | **8046**

COURTYARD

LA REINA

Bed: **5** Bath: **4-1/2**

Width: **80'0"**

Depth: **96'0"**

Level One: **2852** sq ft

Level Two: **969** sq ft

Bonus Room: **330** sq ft

Living Area: **4151** sq ft

Exterior Wall: **2x6**

Foundation: slab

SATER DESIGN PLAN

See price index pages 186-187

65

Tuscan | 8068
VILLA-STYLE
VILLA SABINA

Stone arches, corbels and cornice details accentuate the façade of this Italian-inspired home, which includes a magnificent limestone-sheathed tower and cupola. The two-story foyer, living and dining rooms invite the outdoors inside through myriad windows and glass-fronted doors. Astute architectural detailing, including several unique ceiling applications, punctuates the design premise of the home.

To the right of the foyer, a stunning staircase ascends to the second-floor loft and guest suites. The kitchen, café and family room open onto an expansive verandah through retreating glass doors. The study and master retreat are adjacent to the foyer, with easy access to the verandah.

On the optional lower level, a fully equipped kitchen and family room transition to the loggia and pool area. The rear façade is a profusion of columns, arches and a balustrade-enhanced loggia, which emphasizes the connection between the interior and outside.

PHOTOGRAPHY: CJ WALKER

DINING ROOM

The two-story dining room is an amalgamation of a striking backlit coffered ceiling and scallop-edged loft overlook. A deep-set art niche and glass-fronted French doors bring more intimate proportions to the room.

FOYER/STAIRS

Tall, arched windows gradually decrease in size as the spiral staircase ascends to the second floor. Scrolled, wrought-iron grillwork adorns the banister, while a beamed and appliqué-enhanced cove ceiling adds balance and depth to the space.

LIVING ROOM

The centerpiece of the living room is the wall of elongated windows and corresponding arched transoms, which offer incredible lake views through an exterior arched opening. The curvature of the bay window is manifest in two column-supported entryways, the ceiling's ornate circular soffit design and in the corbel-enhanced fireplace façade.

KITCHEN

While the centerpiece of the European-styled kitchen is the appliqué-and-listello-embellished cut-stone hood, the center preparation island, expansive breakfast bar, custom cabinetry and stunningly tiled backsplash all play an important roll in the overall design.

FOYER/BAR

Framed by two large columns, the centrally located wet bar unites the formal living and dining rooms with the adjacent kitchen and leisure room. An intimate wine cellar is discreetly tucked away under the winding staircase.

MASTER BEDROOM

In addition to the spectacular bathroom and enormous closets, the luxurious master suite boasts a morning kitchen and a spacious sitting room, which opens onto the covered verandah. To spatially differentiate the room, a unique, quadruple-tiered step ceiling cloaks the sitting area, while a triple-tiered coffered ceiling blankets the bedroom area.

MASTER BATH

Floor-to-ceiling, veneered limestone walls complement the stone flooring and decorative cast-stone tiles that surround the tub and vanities. Dual reflections of his and her vanities, with their custom milled cabinetry, are captured in the separate mirrors, adding depth to the room.

OFFICE/STUDY

A pair of French doors invites guests into the masculine study. A series of custom-designed built-ins have been superbly fitted into a wall of three arched niches. The fireplace, with its hand-cut, arched marble façade, comes to life against the textured, suede walls.

MASTER BATH

The focal point of the gloriously appointed master bath is the elevated tub, which is enhanced by two intricately tiled steps, a pair of decorative columns and an arched stone wall. A triptych of windows draws the eye outward to the private garden. A three-panel coffered ceiling complements the window configuration.

LOWER LEVEL

The lower level, which opens to the back-yard and pool, epitomizes what is common-ly referred to as an "open floor plan." Although there are no conventional walls, each room is spatially defined by a collabo-ration of uniquely different and ambitious ceiling treatments, alternating flooring patterns and a compilation of architectural detailing, including a knee wall and numerous columns.

GAME ROOM

A spiral staircase descends to the lower level, which boasts an enormous game room large enough for a variety of concurrent activities. An expansive bay-shaped wall of large paned windows reinforces the eternal connection between the indoors and outdoors.

MAIN FLOOR DECK

Easily accessible from the master suite, study, leisure room, living and dining rooms, the wraparound covered loggia offers a multitude of seating venues, as well as a fully equipped summer kitchen. Simply put, the views will take your breath away.

REAR VIEW

This home is all about being outdoors. With their decorative balustrades and columns, the first-floor and lower-level loggias are within reach of almost every room in the house. The second-story guest wing has a private sun deck.

POWDER BATH

With its delicately blended metallic walls, the luxurious powder room emanates a golden-bronze shimmer. The finishing touch is an ornately carved furniture piece, which is blanketed with a slab of marble and topped with a hammered-copper sink.

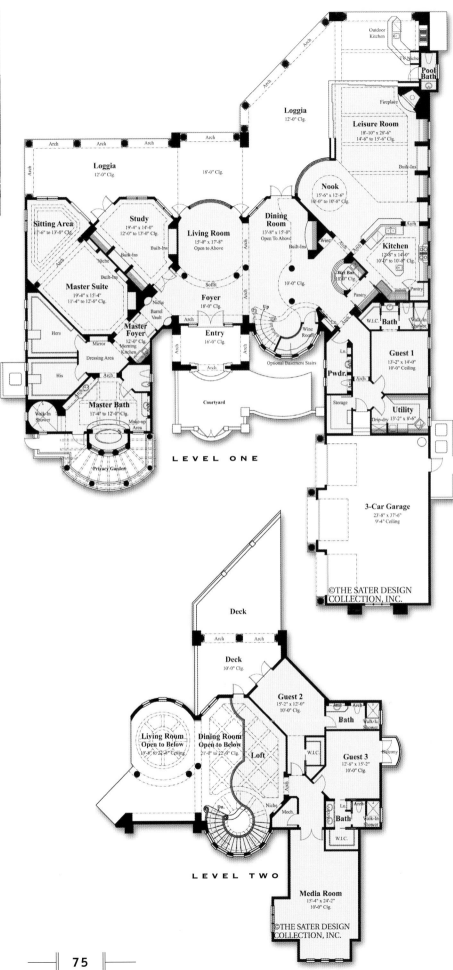

LEVEL ONE

©THE SATER DESIGN COLLECTION, INC.

LEVEL TWO

©THE SATER DESIGN COLLECTION, INC.

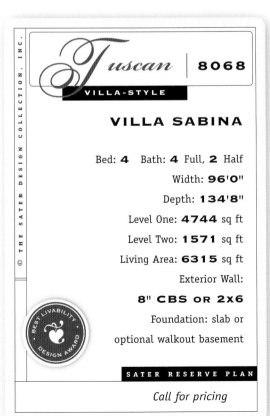

Tuscan | 8068

VILLA-STYLE

VILLA SABINA

Bed: **4**   Bath: **4** Full, **2** Half

Width: **96'0"**

Depth: **134'8"**

Level One: **4744** sq ft

Level Two: **1571** sq ft

Living Area: **6315** sq ft

Exterior Wall:

8" CBS OR 2X6

Foundation: slab or

optional walkout basement

SATER RESERVE PLAN

Call for pricing

© THE SATER DESIGN COLLECTION, INC.

French | **8034**

CHATEAUX

WINTHROP

Sculpted corbels and repeating arches conceal a 21st-century interior tied to its French provenance with ornate millwork, chic moldings, cornices and angled arcades. The integrity of the design is further enhanced by coffered and stepped ceiling treatments, and slender, vertical windows with transoms.

A highly sophisticated arrangement of public and private rooms allows a graceful flow to envelop the home. At the center of the plan, the foyer, formal living and dining rooms converge into one open space, with steppped ceilings providing subtle definition to the rooms. Retreating glass walls extend the living space to the lanai.

Convenient for alfresco meals, the leisure room also features retreating glass walls, blurring the inside/outside relationship with an outdoor-kitchen area of the lanai. Authentic detailing plays in harmony with cutting-edge technology throughout the home.

DINING ROOM

Balance, harmony and grand scale are seen throughout the home, beginning in the formal dining area, where the soaring stepped ceiling is counterbalanced by delicate architectural details found in the built-in buffet.

PHOTOGRAPHY: WILLIAM MINARICH

LIVING ROOM

The centerpiece of the formal living room is the grand hearth, with its ornately carved mantel supported by decorative corbels. Retreating glass doors bring in views of the outdoors and expand the living space to the lanai.

LEISURE ROOM

Flexible spaces that easily adapt to the owner's lifestyle—the kitchen, nook and leisure room—gracefully flow into one common living space. Stepped ceilings provide subtle definition to the rooms.

KITCHEN

Centrally located between the public spaces and informal rooms, the gourmet-caliber kitchen is designed to easily serve both. A center prep island, wraparound eating bar, and plenty of storage and counterspace meld style with function.

NOOK

Sitting under a circular stepped ceiling, curved-glass bay windows envelop the breakfast nook with a panoramic vista of the lanai.

REAR DECK VIEW

Retreating glass doors and multiple sets of windows integrate the interior with the expansive outdoor living spaces. An outdoor kitchen ensures easy entertaining for the homeowner, while friends and family enjoy the pool.

MASTER BEDROOM

Past the double-door entry, the master suite is a four-star retreat. A morning kitchen, dual walk-in closets, luxe bath, sitting nook and sliding glass doors to the lanai create a haven from the hectic pace of everyday life.

MASTER BATH

Symmetrical arches add grace, serenity and splendor to a master bath complete with an oversize whirlpool tub and walk-in shower. To enhance the spa-like experience, multiple windows bring in views of the private garden.

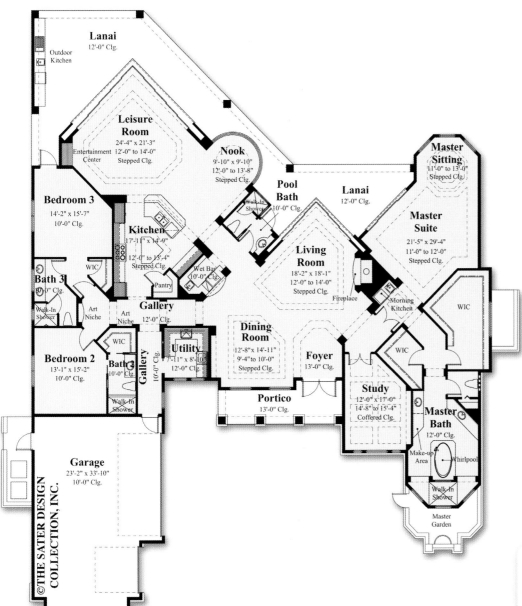

Floor plan labels: Lanai 12'-0" Clg., Outdoor Kitchen, Leisure Room 24'-4" x 21'-3" Entertainment Center 12'-0" to 14'-0" Stepped Clg., Nook 9'-10" x 9'-10" 12'-0" to 13'-8" Stepped Clg., Master Sitting 11'-0" to 13'-0" Stepped Clg., Bedroom 3 14'-2" x 15'-7" 10'-0" Clg., Kitchen 17'-11" x 14'-9" 12'-0" to 13'-4" Stepped Clg., Pool Bath 10'-0" Clg., Lanai 12'-0" Clg., Master Suite 21'-5" x 29'-4" 11'-0" to 12'-0" Stepped Clg., Living Room 18'-2" x 18'-1" 12'-0" to 14'-0" Stepped Clg., Fireplace, Bath 3, WIC, Art Niche, Gallery 12'-0" Clg., Wet Bar 10'-0" Clg., Pantry, Morning Kitchen, WIC, Dining Room 12'-8" x 14'-11" 9'-4" to 10'-0" Stepped Clg., Foyer 13'-0" Clg., WIC, Bedroom 2 13'-1" x 15'-2" 10'-0" Clg., Bath 2, Utility 7'-11" x 8' 12'-0" Clg., Walk-In Shower, Portico 13'-0" Clg., Study 14'-8" to 15'-4" Coffered Clg., Master Bath 12'-0" Clg., Make-up Area, Whirlpool, Walk In Shower, Master Garden, Garage 23'-2" x 33'-10" 10'-0" Clg. ©THE SATER DESIGN COLLECTION, INC.

POWDER BATH

Located between the formal and informal living spaces, this guest bathroom doubles as a pool bath that is easily accessible from the lanai.

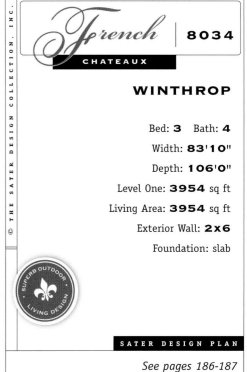

French | **8034**
CHATEAUX

WINTHROP

Bed: **3** Bath: **4**
Width: **83'10"**
Depth: **106'0"**
Level One: **3954** sq ft
Living Area: **3954** sq ft
Exterior Wall: **2x6**
Foundation: slab

SATER DESIGN PLAN

See pages 186-187

Italian | 8076

VILLA-STYLE

LA SERENA

Hipped rooflines, carved eave brackets and varied gables evoke a sense of the past in this Italian-style design. Inside, an engaging blend of old and new prevails where beamed and coffered ceilings play counterpoint to modern amenities—cutting-edge appliances in the kitchen, a state-of-the-art utility room and retreating glass doors in the leisure room.

Past the dramatic entryway, columns line the formal rooms and foyer. The hand-carved fireplace is nestled between built-in cabinetry and lies underneath the cove-lit coffered ceiling. Nearby, the common living space is an open and comfortable retreat with retreating glass doors opening to the lanai. A fun-filled game room lies just beyond the art-niche foyer.

A split-bedroom floor plan provides privacy to the master wing of the home. A generous walk-in closet offers ample storage while the master bath provides a quiet retreat with "his-and-her" vanities, a spa-style tub and walk-in shower.

PHOTOGRAPHY:
CJ WALKER/BRYNN BRUIJN

FOYER ENTRY

Light streams in to the foyer through the sleek curved sidelights surrounding the elegant paneled door. Stone columns and arches define the space, creating a fluid movement into the formal rooms.

LIVING ROOM

Hand-carved Crema Maya stone columns, weighing over one-ton apiece, line the formal living room and foyer. A stunning focal point, the hand-carved fireplace surround is nestled between built-in cabinetry and lies underneath the cove-lit coffered ceiling.

LEISURE ROOM

Sitting under an octagonal coffered ceiling, the leisure room is a comfortable retreat for family and guests. Centrally located between the main living areas, the kitchen promises snacks that are just a few feet away. Retreating glass doors open up to the lanai—making indoor/outdoor entertaining a breeze.

NOOK

Beveled glass surrounds the breakfast nook, and brings the outdoors in (without the bugs). From the nook are clear views of the outdoor fireplace featuring hand-painted mosaic-tile and Crema Maya stone. Repeating arches and columns line the spacious veranda.

KITCHEN

The "heart of the home"—the kitchen features a step-up tray ceiling, spacious pantry, state-of-the-art appliances, a convenient island workstation and an open counter connecting to the leisure room.

VERANDA

Accessible from master bedroom, formal living, leisure and game rooms, the lanai features amenities designed for entertaining and relaxing. The infinity-edge pool includes a secluded spa area, and an outdoor fireplace provides a cozy spot for conversation.

DINING ROOM

Perfect for formal meals, this elegant dining room is adorned with a built-in niche and stepped ceiling. Moonlight pours in through the sunburst-arch transom, creating a romantic and intimate ambiance in the open room.

MASTER BATH

To create a warm and organic feel, earth-toned slate tiles flow throughout the entire master bath. A cove-lit tray ceiling, "his-and-her" vanities, spa-style tub and walk-in shower complete the luxurious retreat.

MASTER CLOSET

Frank Lloyd Wright windows bring light into the generous master walk-in closet. Located next to the master bath, this efficiently designed space provides ample amounts of storage.

MASTER BEDROOM

A split-bedroom floor plan provides privacy to the master wing of the home. Muted lighting creates a relaxing environment, while the sitting nook provides a quiet spot for reading. A step-tray ceiling adds an elegant touch to the spacious room.

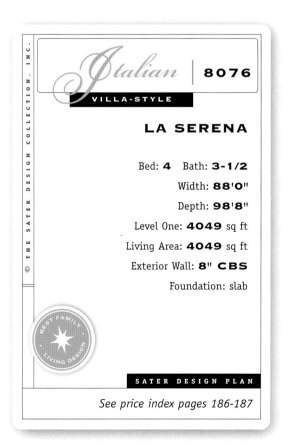

Italian | **8076**

VILLA-STYLE

LA SERENA

Bed: **4**   Bath: **3-1/2**

Width: **88'0"**

Depth: **98'8"**

Level One: **4049** sq ft

Living Area: **4049** sq ft

Exterior Wall: **8" CBS**

Foundation: **slab**

SATER DESIGN PLAN

See price index pages 186-187

English | 8070
BRITISH COLONIAL
LEIGHTON

Quiet elegance is found throughout *Leighton*, a stunning British Colonial home that boasts multiple outdoor living spaces, specialty ceiling treatments and state-of-the-art amenities. Details both romantic and practical are found around every corner—from the living room's striking bow windows to the prodigious use of columns and arched doorways.

A soaring portico and grand turret create an unforgettable façade. Inside, the foyer opens to views of a grand staircase, formal dining room and a wide-open living room that is as impressive for its soaring two-story ceiling as it is for its gorgeously detailed fireplace.

But *Leighton's* pleasures don't end there. You'll find luxurious amenities throughout the private and expansive master suite, the stunning kitchen that opens up to a comfy and exciting leisure room, and the majestic views found in the plan's upstairs bedrooms, balconies and loft.

REAR VIEW

With so many sets of windows commanding views and natural light, the interior naturally extends to multiple outdoor living areas, including a pool overlooked by the guest suite's private balcony.

PHOTOGRAPHY: CJ WALKER

LIVING ROOM

The formal living room, with its dramatic two-story coffered ceiling, is filled with light and views thanks to the abundant bow windows displaying the home's outdoor living areas. The striking fireplace, crafted in handsome detail, provides a grand and comfortable centerpiece.

OUTDOOR KITCHEN

Whether your plans include entertaining friends and family or simply a quiet evening alone, the Leighton design extends the interior to several outdoor living areas. A fully equipped kitchen, roaring fireplace and many intimate details help set the scene.

WET BAR

Set off by graceful arched entryways, the wet bar provides versatility and convenience in joining the home's formal dining room on one side with its kitchen, nook and leisure room on the other.

DINING ROOM

Just inside the foyer, the intimate dining room is defined by stately columns and a tray ceiling. This creates an open, but warm gathering place conveniently located near the wet bar and kitchen.

KITCHEN

From late-night snacks to full-scale dinner parties, the kitchen is where it all happens. This open design includes a wraparound eating bar and provides quick and easy access to the home's large leisure room and nook. A center island with prep sink provides another helpful advantage.

COURTYARD

An outdoor fireplace provides the perfect setting for enjoying meals al fresco by the pool. Glass doors in several rooms open to the cozy outdoor living area.

KITCHEN/LEISURE ROOM

The kitchen, leisure room and nook all come together and provide a wide-open living area for everyone to enjoy. Overlooking the common living space, a generous second-floor loft provides a versatile area that can easily adapt to the owner's lifestyle.

MASTER BEDROOM

The master suite combines exquisite elegance with quiet solitude, creating a welcome retreat. Resplendent in its details, the suite features a step-up tray ceiling, arched entryways with stately columns with access to the veranda and beyond.

LEVEL ONE

©THE Sater DESIGN COLLECTION, INC.

LEVEL TWO

OPTIONAL 5TH BEDROOM

Opt. Bedroom 5
17'-2" x 14'-2"
10'-0" to 12'-0"
Tray Clg.

©THE SATER DESIGN COLLECTION, INC.

MASTER BATH

To create a romantic ambiance, the luxurious master bath is flooded with views from wide, beautiful windows with arched transoms over the whirlpool tub.

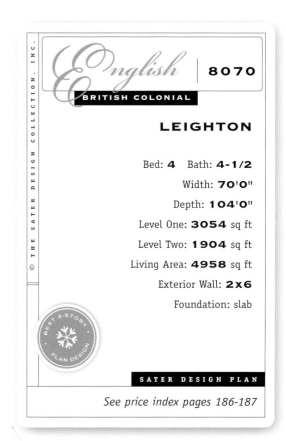

English | **8070**

BRITISH COLONIAL

LEIGHTON

Bed: **4**   Bath: **4-1/2**

Width: **70'0"**

Depth: **104'0"**

Level One: **3054** sq ft

Level Two: **1904** sq ft

Living Area: **4958** sq ft

Exterior Wall: **2x6**

Foundation: **slab**

SATER DESIGN PLAN

See price index pages 186-187

© THE SATER DESIGN COLLECTION, INC.

Spanish | 6947
COLONIAL
SANCHO

STUDY

Optional "his" and "hers" studies feature custom-wood built-ins, wrought-iron accents and access to the loggia through double doors.

The influence of Spanish Colonial-style is clearly evident in this rambling home that truly welcomes the outside in. Lush planters greet visitors as they enter an engaging entry turret made even grander by a decorative, second-story, wrought-iron balcony. Further accenting the great outdoors is an expansive covered loggia that wraps the rear elevation.

Inside, this home is all about luxurious and relaxed living, with rooms that exceed expectation in both design and function. The gourmet-caliber kitchen resides under an octagonal-shaped ceiling and is adjacent to the leisure room and breakfast nook. This combination space is the hub of the home, perfect for intimate family gatherings and large-scale entertaining. Parties flow easily outside, through two walls of pocketing glass doors framing the leisure room and connecting to a rambling loggia that has its own entertainment center—a solana and outdoor kitchen.

FOYER

True luxury is in the details—wrought-iron accents enhance built-in arches and rough-hewn wood beams add an Old-World touch to the stepped ceiling of this uniquely designed foyer. Guests can be ushered straight through the foyer to the loggia through sliding glass doors or to the formal dining room.

KITCHEN

With spacious swirled-granite countertops, ample storage space and a convenient butcher-block center island, this octagonal-shaped gourmet kitchen is friendly to chefs, family and friends alike.

DINING ROOM

Located directly off of the foyer, soft lighting makes the faux-painted walls of the formal dining room glow under the beamed octagonal-shaped ceiling. Tall bay windows perfectly frame a sunset, and a built-in niche provides sophisticated display space for favorite pieces of fine art.

LEISURE ROOM

The leisure room is infused with warmth, granted by hand-hewn media cabinetry, ceiling beams and a connection to an intimate butterfly garden just beyond the French doors. Retreating glass doors open the opposite side of the room to the solana and loggia.

MASTER BEDROOM

An elegant bedroom with a bay-windowed sitting area is at the core of a sprawling master suite. The retreat also boasts dual walk-in closets (one with a stacked washer and dryer), a study and spa-like bath.

OUTDOOR LIVING

A charming chiminea-style fireplace warms the outdoor kitchen and adjacent sitting area. Just steps from the leisure room and "her" study, this outdoor room is perfect for a lively party or a soothing cup of tea.

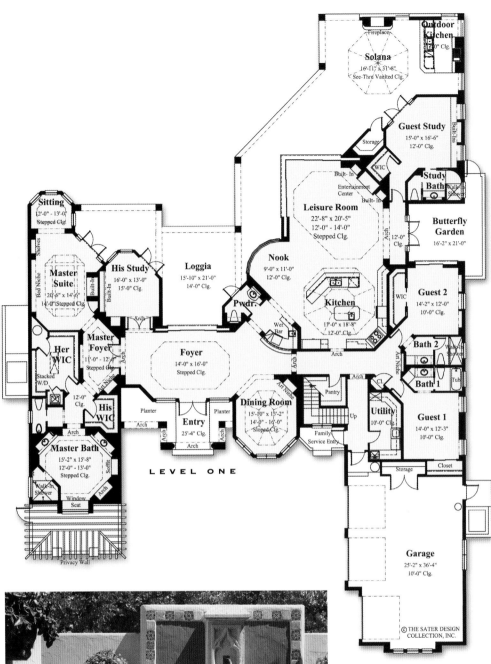

LEVEL ONE

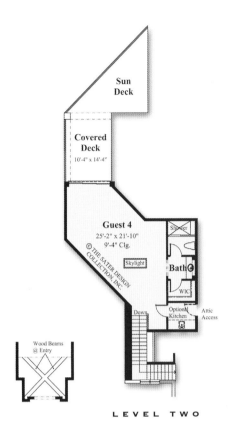

LEVEL TWO

BUTTERFLY GARDEN

A streaming fountain adds natural music to a butterfly garden adjoining the leisure room and guest room. This cozy space provides an ideal retreat from a hectic day.

Spanish | **6947**

COLOLNIAL

SANCHO

Bed: **4**   Bath: **5-1/2**

Width: **95'0"**

Depth: **134'6"**

Level One: **4716** sq ft

Level Two: **619** sq ft

Living Area: **5335** sq ft

Exterior Wall: **8" CBS**

Foundation: slab

SATER DESIGN PLAN

See price index pages 186-187

Italian | **8025**
VILLA-STYLE
VASARI

A stunning window-lined turret, classic columns and repeating arches create a striking façade. An uninhibited spirit prevails within—where a gallery foyer and loft deepen the central living/dining room, allowing a stepped ceiling to soar above open vistas defined only by decorative columns. A two-sided fireplace warms the central area as well as a study that boasts a private porch.

A view-oriented leisure room enjoys multiple connections with the outdoors. The openness of the kitchen/nook/leisure rooms creates a flexible, informal area that is perfect for spending time with friends and family.

Above the entry, a sun porch with French doors permits sunlight to invigorate the loft—an inviting space that connects the family's sleeping quarters with a private guest suite. The main level brags a cabana-style guest suite, with access to a compartmented bath and shower from the veranda.

FOYER ENTRY

Designed to provide a warm welcome for friends and family, the gallery foyer is bathed in light streaming in through its double doors. Decorative wrought-iron railing flows up the stairs in the glass-encased turret to the loft overlooking the well-appointed formal rooms.

PHOTOGRAPHY: RICHARD LEO JOHNSON —— 100 ——

ENTRY HALL

The gallery foyer leads to a library/study at one end and provides passage to the common living areas at the other. An elevator (white paneled door at right in photo) is a convenient and popular option in this plan.

KITCHEN

The kitchen is no longer just for cooking—
it's where everyone gathers and where
favorite moments are shared. That means
the kitchen must be open, unrestrained by
walls, free to spill out into other areas
just like guests do when you're entertaining or hosting family events.

LIVING ROOM

In the formal living/dining room, floor-to-ceiling windows offer commanding views of the veranda and beyond. A two-story stepped ceiling soars over the area, adding a perfect touch of drama. Mixing style with function, a two-sided fireplace—shared with the adjacent library/study—provides warmth and beauty.

ENTRY

A small peek through the entryway is an invitation to the formal living area and on through to the outside. Everywhere you step in this home, you can feel how open it is, as if you're flowing through it.

MASTER BEDROOM

Vasari *has been created with gathering, vacationing and entertaining in mind— but it can also be for escaping. The plan's master retreat includes its own foyer and porch, ideal for seeking impressive, secluded refuge while still remaining under the same roof.*

MASTER BATH

The plan's master retreat is rounded out by a master bath—including whirlpool tub and walk-in shower—also accessed by its own foyer, as well as a massive, two-sided, walk-in closet.

Options for comfortable gathering abound throughout the plan's open kitchen area, breakfast nook and leisure room. Arched doorways provide access to the veranda, pool, shore and beyond.

REAR VIEW

The villa-style of Vasari *is perhaps most apparent in its "s" tile roof and romantic-arched verandah and balcony. (Shown with optional extended verandah and outdoor cabana.)*

REAR DECK

This home offers the perfect option for taking advantage of a quality piece of land—especially those located close to the shoreline. Vasari *merges the beauty of the outside with the ingenuity of any inside you care to create.*

MASTER WARDROBE

The perfect place to display treasured purses and shoes, the master closet offers generous amounts of storage space. To make it even more convenient, the homeowners chose to modify the plan to open the closet into the master bath.

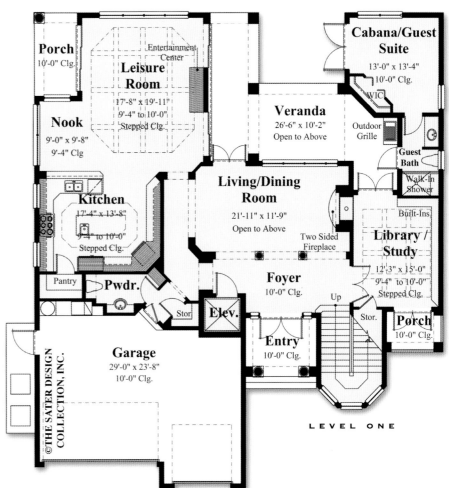

LEVEL ONE

©THE SATER DESIGN COLLECTION, INC.

- **Porch** 10'-0" Clg.
- Entertainment Center
- **Leisure Room** 17'-8" x 19'-11" 9'-4" to 10'-0" Stepped Clg.
- **Nook** 9'-0" x 9'-8" 9'-4" Clg.
- **Kitchen** 17'-4" x 13'-8" 9'-4" to 10'-0" Stepped Clg.
- Pantry
- **Pwdr.**
- **Garage** 29'-0" x 23'-8" 10'-0" Clg.
- **Cabana/Guest Suite** 13'-0" x 13'-4" 10'-0" Clg.
- WIC
- **Veranda** 26'-6" x 10'-2" Open to Above
- Outdoor Grille
- **Guest Bath**
- Walk-In Shower
- **Living/Dining Room** 21'-11" x 11'-9" Open to Above
- Two Sided Fireplace
- Built-Ins
- **Library / Study** 12'-3" x 15'-0" 9'-4" to 10'-0" Stepped Clg.
- **Foyer** 10'-0" Clg.
- Stor.
- **Elev.**
- Up
- Stor.
- **Porch** 10'-0" Clg.
- **Entry** 10'-0" Clg.

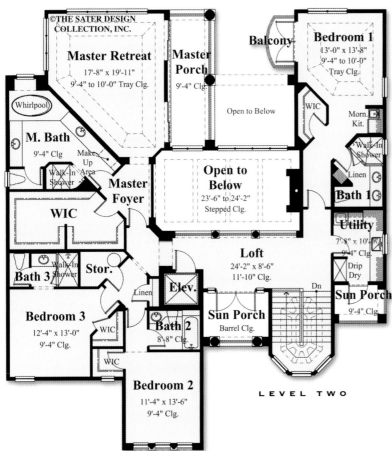

LEVEL TWO

©THE SATER DESIGN COLLECTION, INC.

- **Master Retreat** 17'-8" x 19'-11" 9'-4" to 10'-0" Tray Clg.
- Whirlpool
- **M. Bath** 9'-4" Clg.
- Make-Up Area
- Walk-In Shower
- **Master Porch** 9'-4" Clg.
- **Balcony**
- **Bedroom 1** 13'-0" x 13'-8" 9'-4" to 10'-0" Tray Clg.
- Open to Below
- WIC
- Morn. Kit.
- Walk-In Shower
- Linen
- **Bath 1**
- **Master Foyer**
- **WIC**
- **Open to Below** 23'-6" to 24'-2" Stepped Clg.
- **Utility** 7'-2" x 10'-?" 9'-4" Clg.
- Drip Dry
- **Bath 3**
- Walk-In Shower
- **Stor.**
- **Elev.**
- Linen
- **Loft** 24'-2" x 8'-6" 11'-10" Clg.
- Dn
- **Sun Porch** 9'-4" Clg.
- **Bedroom 3** 12'-4" x 13'-0" 9'-4" Clg.
- WIC
- **Bath 2** 8'-8" Clg.
- **Sun Porch** Barrel Clg.
- WIC
- **Bedroom 2** 11'-4" x 13'-6" 9'-4" Clg.

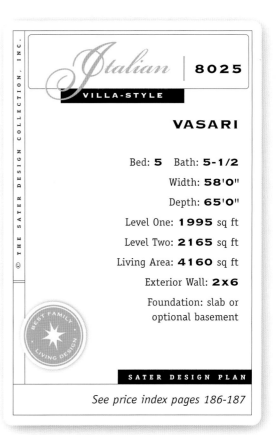

Italian | **8025**

VILLA-STYLE

VASARI

Bed: **5**   Bath: **5-1/2**

Width: **58'0"**

Depth: **65'0"**

Level One: **1995** sq ft

Level Two: **2165** sq ft

Living Area: **4160** sq ft

Exterior Wall: **2x6**

Foundation: slab or optional basement

© THE SATER DESIGN COLLECTION, INC.

BEST FAMILY LIVING DESIGN

SATER DESIGN PLAN

See price index pages 186-187

Tuscan | **6786**
COURTYARD
FERRETTI

With its terracotta-hued barrel roof tiles, stone-clad walls, stone accents and golden-hued stucco façade, this is the quintessential Tuscan-inspired home. A pair of wrought-iron gates opens to the courtyard and leads to a loggia of stone-covered pillars and arched openings that travels the length of the home. Myriad windows and glass doors grace the interior walls, connecting the interior and exterior spaces.

To the left of the foyer, the master suite faces the pool and seemingly draws the outdoors in. The library is located near the foyer and adjacent to the airy kitchen, dining and great room, which naturally transition outward onto the covered loggia and pool area. Facing the enclosed courtyard, two second-story guest suites share a common loft that opens onto a covered balcony and pergola-shaded deck. Anchored on one side by a private guesthouse, the courtyard, with its privacy wall and fountain, enhances the home's oasis-like ambiance.

COURTYARD ENTRY

Limestone-sheathed pillars and arched openings form a loggia that travels the length of the home from the portico to the main entry. The master suite faces the pool, emphasizing the fundamental synthesis of the indoor and outdoor environments.

GREAT ROOM

Adjacent to the dining room and kitchen, the great room—with its matching built-ins, wood-beamed ceiling and wood mantel fireplace—ties together like a perfectly accessorized outfit. A pair of ornately scrolled iron-grilled windows, complement the beautiful millwork.

KITCHEN

The spacious kitchen and dining area, with its large center island and extended break-fast bar, transitions easily into the great room, which opens onto the covered lanai and subsequent pool deck. To the left, French doors lead to an intimate study.

MASTER BEDROOM

An expansive wall of glass-fronted doors connects the master suite—with its softly hued walls and elegantly tiered ceiling—to the stunningly designed pool and spa area. A high wall encircles one side of the court-yard ensuring complete privacy.

GREAT ROOM

A wall of sliding glass doors expose a tranquil courtyard setting, complete with an outdoor kitchen, wall fountain and pool with spa. Slump arches and a rough-hewn beamed ceiling define the public areas. To the other side of the great room is easy access to a powder bath and the second floor loft and two guest suites.

COURTYARD VIEW

Essential to the home's design is the visual and physical associations that connect each interior space to the outdoors, including the detached guesthouse and second-story guest wing. Astute architectural detailing, such as the gently sloped roofline, decorative pergola and column-enhanced and beamed balcony ceiling, strengthens the relationship between the home and its surroundings. Framed on two sides by a covered walkway, the ascetically landscaped pool and spa enhance the courtyard's tranquil, oasis-like ambiance.

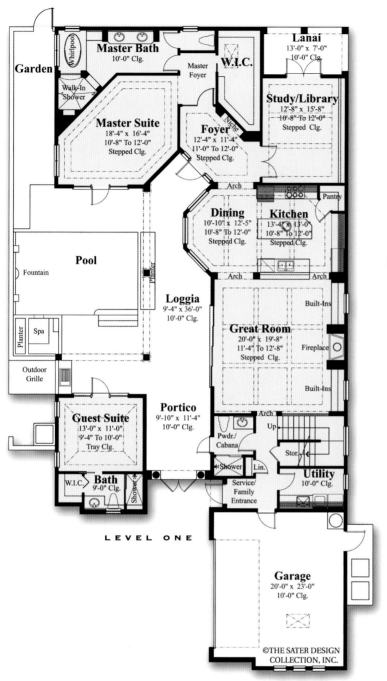

LEVEL ONE

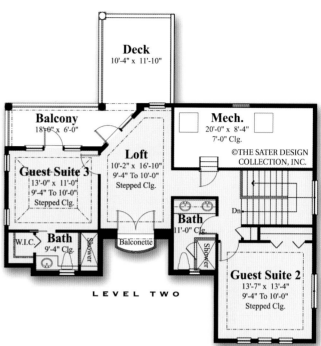

LEVEL TWO

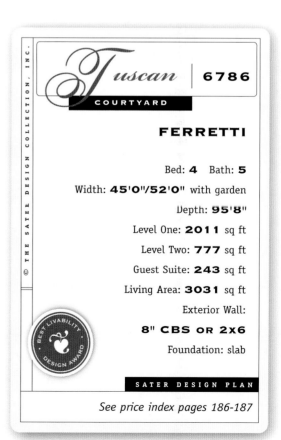

©THE SATER DESIGN COLLECTION, INC.

GUEST SUITE

An opulent retreat for visiting friends and family, the detached guest suite offers a quiet place to relax. Accessible from the courtyard, the private suite features a step-up tray ceiling, walk-in closet and full bath.

Tuscan | 6786
COURTYARD

FERRETTI

Bed: **4**   Bath: **5**

Width: **45'0"/52'0"** with garden

Depth: **95'8"**

Level One: **2011** sq ft

Level Two: **777** sq ft

Guest Suite: **243** sq ft

Living Area: **3031** sq ft

Exterior Wall:

8" CBS OR 2X6

Foundation: slab

SATER DESIGN PLAN

See price index pages 186-187

8068 VILLA SABINA

Tuscan Steeped in a profoundly elegant, rich history, Tuscan homes are textured with natural beauty and exude a unique sense of strength and style. Stone, iron and rough-hewn wood join together and envelope you in a Renaissance-like feeling of artistic wonder. The stunning and enduring stone exteriors— accented by columns, arches and classic gables—give way to generous and handsome rooms of convenience, warmth and comfort. Gourmet kitchens that lead into formal dining rooms and family-style great rooms; secluded master suites that offer peaceful respite in exquisite style; balconies and verandahs that extend outward to reveal fabulous sun decks, terraces and balconies—these are the hallmarks of a Tuscan home's timeless rustic allure.

REAR VIEW

© THE SATER DESIGN COLLECTION, INC.

WWW.EUROPEANHOUSEPLANS.COM

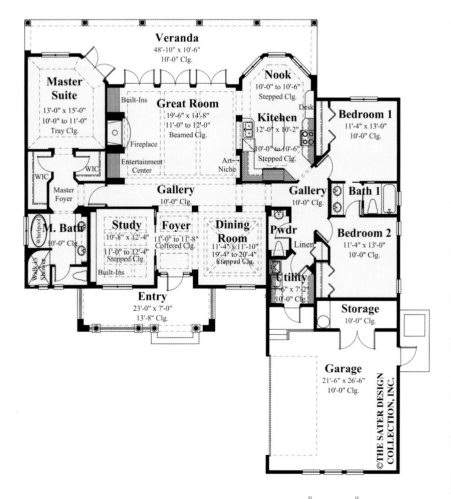

© THE SATER DESIGN COLLECTION, INC.

Tuscan | **8071**

VILLA

CASINA ROSSA

Columns, stucco and rough-hewn stone embellish the façade of this charming Tuscan villa. Inside, a beamed ceiling contributes a sense of spaciousness to the heart of the home, while walls of glass draw the outdoors inside. Varied ceiling treatments and sculpted arches define the wide-open interior, permitting flexibility as well as great views. The great room is anchored by a massive fireplace flanked by built-in shelves and an entertainment center—visible from the kitchen via a pass-thru.

Bed: **3** Bath: **2-1/2**

Width: **62'10"** Depth: **73'6"**

Level One: **2191** sq ft

Living Area: **2191** sq ft

Exterior Wall: **2x6**

Foundation: slab or optional basement

BEST 1-STORY PLAN DESIGN

SATER DESIGN PLAN

See price index pages 186-187

© THE SATER DESIGN COLLECTION, INC.

www.europeanhouseplans.com © THE SATER DESIGN COLLECTION, INC.

REAR VIEW

Tuscan | 8069
VILLA

DOMENICO

Past the magnificent portico entry, columns and arches define the formal spaces designed for greeting and entertaining guests, with a wet bar providing refreshments. To the rear of the plan, the leisure room flows onto the solana and loggia, with a nearby Cabana offering a perfect retreat for guests. On the opposite wing, the master suite opens to a private pavilion. Upstairs, friends and family will enjoy the clubroom, wet bar and state-of-the-art theater room.

Bed: **4** Bath: **4** Full, **2** Half

Width: **92'0"** Depth: **157'3"**

Level One: **4309** sq ft

Level Two: **1417** sq ft

Cabana: **400** sq ft

Living Area: **6126** sq ft

Exterior Wall: **8" CBS**

Foundation: slab

SATER RESERVE PLAN

Call for pricing

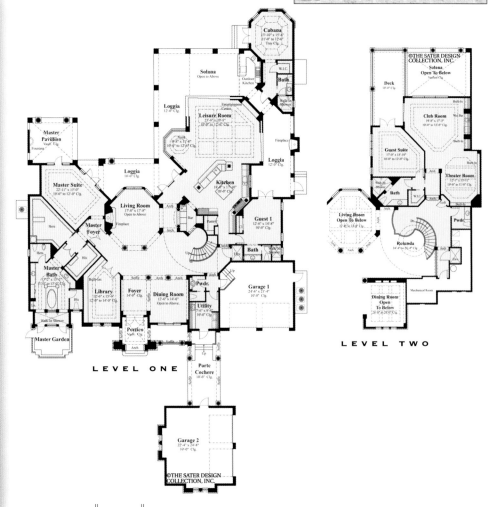

LEVEL ONE

LEVEL TWO

COURTYARD VIEW

© THE SATER DESIGN COLLECTION, INC.

WWW.EUROPEANHOUSEPLANS.COM

Mech.
11'-2" x 13'-2"
9'-4" Clg.

Study
19'-6" x 13'-0"
9'-4" to 10'-2"
Stepped Clg.

Built-Ins

Deck
8'-6" x 18'-8"

Open To Below

Loft
11'-6" to 17'-10"
9'-4" to 10'-2"
Stepped Clg.

Balcony
20'-0" x 5'-8"
9'-4" Clg.

9'-4" Clg.

Bath 2
9'-4" Clg.

Guest Suite 3
13'-8" x 12'-0"
9'-4" to 10'-2"
Tray Clg.

Stairwell
10'-4" x 13'-10"
Stepped Clg.

Bath 3
W.I.C.   9'-4" Clg.

Guest Suite 2
11'-2" x 14'-0"
9'-4" Clg.

©THE SATER DESIGN
COLLECTION, INC.

LEVEL TWO

Lanai
11'-8" x 10'-0"
10'-0" Clg.

Arch

Built-Ins   Built-Ins

Living Room
15'-0" x 18'-4"
10'-8" to 12'-0"
Stepped Clg.

Fireplace

W.I.C.

Walk-In Shower

Master Bath
10'-2" x 15'-2"
10'-0" to 11'-0"
Stepped Clg.

Whirlpool

Garden

Dining
11'-2" x 15'-2"
10'-8" to 12'-0"
Stepped Clg.

Arch

Foyer
15'-0" x 6'-0"
10'-8" Clg.

Arch   Arch

Master Bedroom
16'-6" x 13'-6"
10'-0" to 12'-0"
Tray Clg.

Deck

Arch

Kitchen
11'-6" x 13'-6"
11'-4" to 12'-0"
Stepped Clg.

Nook
9'-4" x 13'-0"
11'-4" to 12'-0"
Stepped Clg.

Arch

Pool

Fountain

Built-Ins

Leisure Room
17'-2" x 17'-8"

Open to Above

10'-0" Clg.

Loggia
13'-8" x 29'-8"
10'-0" Clg.

Arch

Arch

Arch

Arch   Outdoor Grille

Portico
6'-6" x 6'-6"
10'-0" Clg.

Guest Suite
13'-8" x 12'-0"
9'-4" to 10'-2"
Tray Clg.

Pwdr. Bath

Utility Room
10'-0" Clg.

Up

Entry
Barrel Vault Clg.

Stor.

W.I.C.

Bath
9'-4" Clg.

Walk-In Shower

Garage
20'-0" x 24'-0"
10'-0" Clg.

©THE SATER DESIGN
COLLECTION, INC

LEVEL ONE

Tuscan | 6787

COURTYARD

SALCITO

This charming courtyard home features spaces filled with Mediterranean design details and open connections to a central loggia. The main-floor leisure room has a two-story, boxed-beamed ceiling, a wall of built-ins and retreating glass doors to the loggia. Nearby, the formal dining and living rooms open to a private lanai. The second level includes a study, guest bedrooms and multiple decks with courtyard views.

Bed: **4**   Bath: **4-1/2**

Width: **45'0"/52'2"** with garden

Depth: **94'0"**

Level One: **2087** sq ft

Level Two: **1099** sq ft

Living Area: **3458** sq ft

Bonus Room: **272** sq ft

Exterior Wall:
8" CBS OR 2x6

Foundation: slab

SUPERB OUTDOOR LIVING DESIGN

SATER DESIGN PLAN

See price index pages 186-187

REAR VIEW

Tuscan | 8075

VILLA

MARGHERITA

This new take on "Tuscan" offers forward-facing stone gables, cast-stone window surrounds and a majestic chimney stack. Inside, entertaining is made easy with built-in cabinetry, a pass-thru wet bar, cutting-edge kitchen appliances, and a standalone media center between the leisure and game rooms. Rounded arches define the transition between rooms and open spaces. Near the rear of the plan, the leisure room opens to the veranda with its dramatic triple arches and outdoor kitchen.

Bed: **4**   Bath: **3-1/2**

Width: **80'0"**   Depth: **104'8"**

Level One: **3752** sq ft

Living Area: **3752** sq ft

Exterior Wall: **2x6**

Foundation: slab or optional basement

BEST 2-STORY PLAN DESIGN

SATER DESIGN PLAN

See price index pages 186-187

OPTIONAL 4TH BEDROOM

REAR VIEW

© THE SATER DESIGN COLLECTION, INC.

Veranda
37'-2" x 12'-8"
12'-0" Clg.

Breakfast
13'-6" x 9'-0"
9'-4" to 10'-0"
Beamed Clg.

Outdoor Grille

Built-Ins

Kitchen
14'-8" x 16'-6"
9'-4" to 10'-0"
Beamed Clg.

©THE SATER DESIGN
COLLECTION, INC.

Great Room
21'-0" x 17'-2"
Open to Above

Fireplace

Master Suite
14'-8" x 17'-0"
12'-0" to 13'-0"
Tray Clg.

WIC

Entertainment Center

Storage

Garage
23'-0" x 24'-0"
10'-2" Clg.

Dn

Up

Art Niche

Master Bath
11'-0" Clg.

Whirlpool

Dining
13'-0" x 12'-0"
9'-0" to 10'-0"
Stepped Clg.

Pantry
8'-8" Clg.

Utility
9'-0" x 6'-4"
9'-0" Clg.

Walk-In Shower

Powder Bath
9'-4" Clg.

Foyer
9'-4" to 10'-0"
Stepped Clg.

Study/Office
13'-0" x 13'-8"
9'-4" to 10'-0"
Beamed Clg.

Portico
10'-0" Clg.

LEVEL ONE

Bedroom 2
13'-0" x 12'-0"
9'-0" Clg.

©THE SATER DESIGN
COLLECTION, INC.

Open to Below
21'-0" to 21'-8"
Coffered Clg.

WIC

WIC

Dn

Bonus Room

Bonus Bath
13'-8" x 14'-0"
Vault to 10'-2"
Clg.

Walk-In Shower

10'-2" Clg.

Bath 1
9'-0" Clg.

Walk-In Shower

Niche

WIC

Bath 2
9'-0" Clg.

Dn

Computer Loft
9'-0" Clg.

WIC

Desk

Bedroom 1
13'-0" x 12'-6"
12'-4" Clg.

Guest Suite
13'-0" x 11'-8"
9'-0" Clg.

Deck

LEVEL TWO

Tuscan | 8004

VILLA

CHADBRYNE

Stacked stone and stucco capture the character of a rural Italian manor. Inside, an open foyer is defined by columns and arches, allowing views that extend past the veranda. Architectural details—a coffered ceiling above the two-story great room, an art niche and built-in cabinetry—contribute to the rusticated decor. Throughout the home state-of-the-art appliances play counterpoint to rough-hewn ceiling beams and stone accents.

Bed: **4**   Bath: **3-1/2**

Width: **91'0"**   Depth: **52'8"**

Level One: **2219** sq ft

Level Two: **1085** sq ft

Living Area: **3304** sq ft

Bonus Room: **404** sq ft

Exterior Wall: **2x6**

Foundation: slab or optional basement

SATER DESIGN PLAN

See price index pages 186-187

WWW.EUROPEANHOUSEPLANS.COM

© THE SATER DESIGN COLLECTION, INC.

REAR VIEW

Tuscan | 8077

COURTYARD

MONTE ROSA

Brackets support a triple set of low-pitched gables clad in Tuscan-style rustic stone. The groin-vaulted portico opens to the courtyard, leading past the shimmering pool to the formal entry of the home. Inside, the foyer opens to the grand room and, through an arched opening, to the formal dining room. Glass bayed walls in the central living area meld interior and outdoor spaces. To the front of the courtyard, a casita offers space that easily converts to a home office.

Bed: **4**   Bath: **4-1/2**

Width: **80'0"**   Depth: **96'2"**

Level One: **2852** sq ft

Level Two: **969** sq ft

Guest Suite: **333** sq ft

Living Area: **4154** sq ft

Exterior Wall: **8" CBS** or **2x6**

Foundation: slab

SATER DESIGN PLAN

See price index pages 186-187

LEVEL ONE

©THE SATER DESIGN COLLECTION, INC.

LEVEL TWO

©THE SATER DESIGN COLLECTION, INC.

REAR VIEW

© THE SATER DESIGN COLLECTION, INC.

WWW.EUROPEANHOUSEPLANS.COM

©THE SATER DESIGN COLLECTION, INC.

Veranda
10'-0" x 18'-6"
10'-8" Clg.

Garage
25'-0" x 22'-0"
12'-0" Clg.

Outdoor Kitchen

Veranda
34'-0" x 13'-8"
14'-8" Clg.

Master Suite
13'-0" x 16'-10"
10'-8" to 12'-8"
Stepped Clg.

WIC

Great Room
19'-6" x 15'-3"
Open to Above

Built-Ins

Fireplace

Built-Ins

Nook
13'-6" x 10'-10"
10'-0" to 10'-8"
Stepped Clg.

Mud Room
7'-8" x 8'-4"
10'-8" Clg.

Kitchen
13'-6" x 13'-4"
10'-0" to 10'-8"
Stepped Clg.

Utility
10'-0" x 7'-5"
10'-8" Clg.

Pantry

Master Foyer

WIC

Master Bath
10'-8" Clg.

Whirlpool

Walk-In Shower

Art Niche

Foyer
10'-8" Clg.

Gallery
10'-8" Clg.

Pwdr.

Up

Study
13'-0" x 14'-2"
10'-0" to 10'-8"
Stepped Clg.

Portico
10'-8" Clg.

Dining Room
13'-0" x 13'-10"
10'-2" to 10'-8"
Coffered Clg.

Friends' Entry
10'-8" Clg.

LEVEL ONE

Guest Deck
10'-0" x 18'-6"

Guest Suite
19'-2" x 13'-0"
9'-0" to 10'-0"
Tray Clg.

Open to Below
21'-4" to 22'-0"
Coffered Clg.

Built-In

W.I.C.

Guest Bath
Walk-In Shower

Stor.
9'-4" Clg.

Walk-In Shower

WIC

Bath 2
9'-4" Clg.

©THE SATER DESIGN COLLECTION, INC.

Loft
9'-4" to 10'-0"
Stepped Clg.

Built-In Desk

Built-In Bookshelves

Bedroom 2
13'-0" x 13'-10"
12'-4" Clg.

Sun Porch
9'-4" Clg.

Bedroom 1
13'-0" x 13'-10"
9'-4" Clg.

Bath 1
9'-4" Clg.

LEVEL TWO

THE SATER DESIGN COLLECTION, INC.

Tuscan | 8020
VILLA RUSTICA

VIENNA

A dialogue between tradition and innovation, the Old-World elements of this striking façade belie a form-and-function interior packed with new-century amenities. Parallel wings harbor private and public realms, connected by an airy great room and gallery-style foyer. An extended-hearth fireplace shares its beauty with the common living zone—the great room, kitchen and nook. A sun porch on the upper level extends light to the loft, linking bedroom suites and guest quarters.

Bed: **4**   Bath: **4-1/2**

Width: **80'0"**   Depth: **63'9"**

Level One: **2232** sq ft

Level Two: **1269** sq ft

Living Area: **3501** sq ft

Exterior Wall: **2x6**

Foundation: slab or optional basement

ELEGANT · LIVING DESIGN ·

SATER DESIGN PLAN

See price index pages 186-187

WWW.EUROPEANHOUSEPLANS.COM © THE SATER DESIGN COLLECTION, INC.

REAR VIEW

Tuscan | **8057**

VILLA

MASSIMO

Colonial lines evoke the ancient forms of the houses of Tuscany, yet this grand manor steps boldly into the present. A side courtyard complements a veranda that wraps around the rear of the plan, bordered by walls of glass. French doors open the central living and dining space to the world outside. Upstairs, guest bedrooms open to a shared deck with rear-property views, while a spacious loft overlooks the living room below.

Bed: **5**   Bath: **4-1/2**

Width: **69'4"**   Depth: **95'4"**

Level One: **2920** sq ft

Level Two: **1478** sq ft

Living Area: **4398** sq ft

Exterior Wall: **2x6**

Foundation: slab or optional basement

SATER DESIGN PLAN

See price index pages 186-187

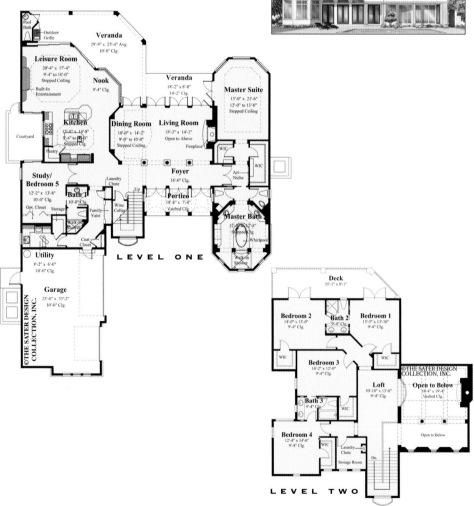

LEVEL ONE

LEVEL TWO

REAR VIEW

© THE SATER DESIGN COLLECTION, INC.

WWW.EUROPEANHOUSEPLANS.COM

© THE SATER DESIGN COLLECTION, INC.

Tuscan | 8059

VILLA URBANA

SIMONE

Stacked-stone gables dramatically define the neighborhood presence of this Italian villa. Beyond the entry, the plan offers well-defined rooms and wide-open spaces, with views of nature everywhere. Columns define the boundaries of the formal dining room, permitting interior vistas as well as easy service from the kitchen. Retreating glass doors provide views and expand the living and leisure rooms onto the spacious lanai, where guests can enjoy meals al fresco by the built-in grille.

Bed: **4**   Bath: **3-1/2**

Width: **67'0"**   Depth: **91'8"**

Level One: **3231** sq ft

Living Area: **3231** sq ft

Exterior Wall:

8" CBS OR 2X6

Foundation: slab

FAMILY-FRIENDLY LIVING DESIGN

SATER DESIGN PLAN

See price index pages 186-187

REAR VIEW

Tuscan | **8063**

VILLA RUSTICA

SANTA TRINITA

Tuscan charm invites a feeling of home outside and in, with floor-to-ceiling windows letting in the sun. The front of the home features formal spaces intended for entertaining with richly textured amenities such as a stone-mantel fireplace, cabinetry and stepped ceilings. To the rear of the plan, the leisure room flows through retreating glass walls onto the lanai. A gallery hall runs the width of the plan, linking three guest bedrooms with the master suite.

Bed: **4**   Bath: **3-1/2**

Width: **68'8"**   Depth: **91'8"**

Level One: **3497** sq ft

Living Area: **3497** sq ft

Exterior Wall: **2x6**

Foundation: slab

SATER DESIGN PLAN

See price index pages 186-187

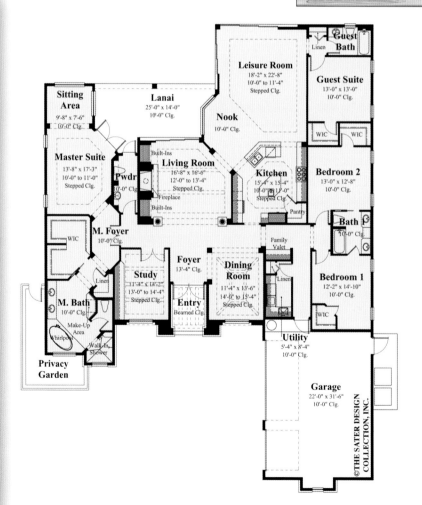

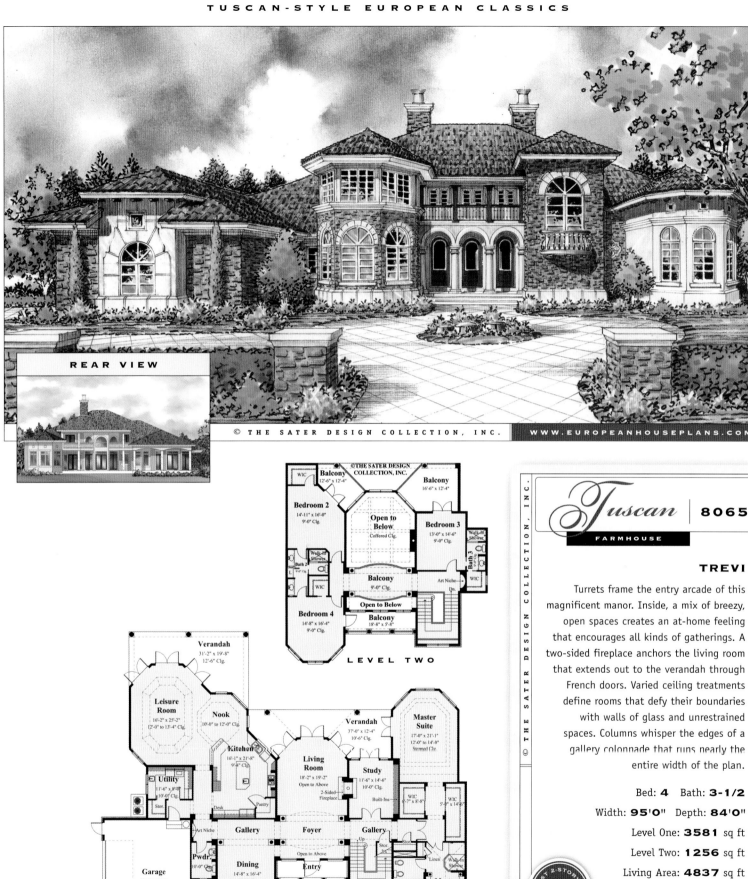

REAR VIEW

© THE SATER DESIGN COLLECTION, INC.

WWW.EUROPEANHOUSEPLANS.COM

©THE SATER DESIGN COLLECTION, INC.

LEVEL TWO

LEVEL ONE

© THE SATER DESIGN COLLECTION, INC.

Juscan | **8065**

FARMHOUSE

TREVI

Turrets frame the entry arcade of this magnificent manor. Inside, a mix of breezy, open spaces creates an at-home feeling that encourages all kinds of gatherings. A two-sided fireplace anchors the living room that extends out to the verandah through French doors. Varied ceiling treatments define rooms that defy their boundaries with walls of glass and unrestrained spaces. Columns whisper the edges of a gallery colonnade that runs nearly the entire width of the plan.

Bed: **4**   Bath: **3-1/2**

Width: **95'0"**   Depth: **84'0"**

Level One: **3581** sq ft

Level Two: **1256** sq ft

Living Area: **4837** sq ft

Exterior Wall: **2x6**

Foundation: basement

BEST 2-STORY PLAN DESIGN

SATER RESERVE PLAN

Call for pricing

8046 LA REINA

Italian

Strong, noble homes crafted with a sense of history, art and romance pay homage to the beauty of the Italian countryside. Grand turrets and columns create exhilarating first impressions while alluring porticos offer invitations to enjoy breathtaking courtyards and foyers. Inside, graceful arches and soaring ceilings create a dramatic, Baroque sensation. Large, plentiful windows stream the midday sun and rooms spill freely out to verandahs and captivating outdoor living areas. From stately and luxurious master suites to generous leisure rooms and open kitchens, these Italian homes are created with an abiding commitment to style, comfort and family.

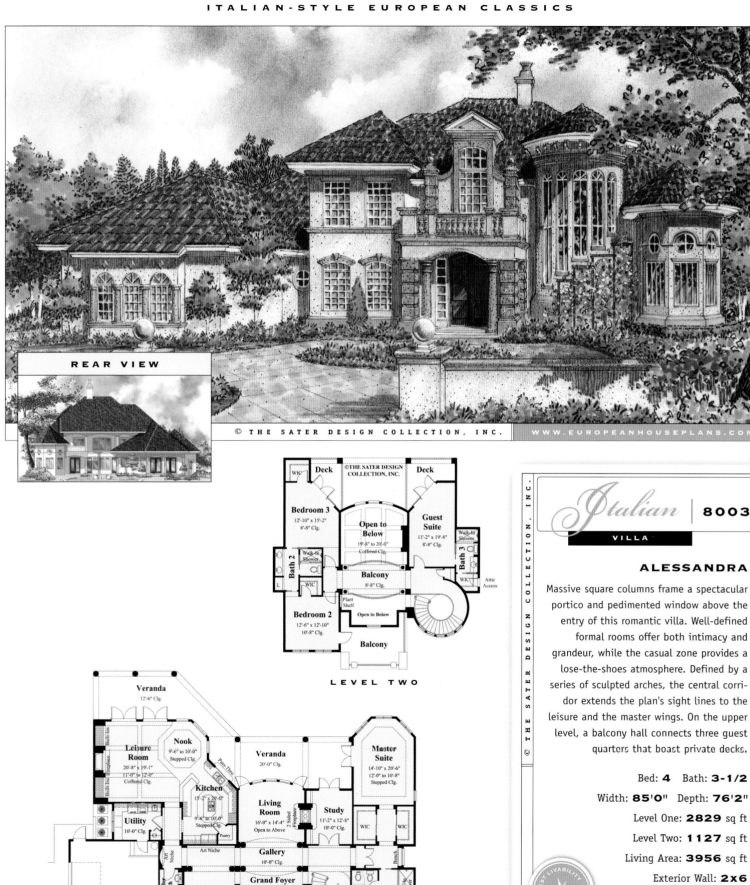

REAR VIEW

© THE SATER DESIGN COLLECTION, INC.

WWW.EUROPEANHOUSEPLANS.COM

LEVEL TWO

WIC

Deck

©THE SATER DESIGN COLLECTION, INC.

Deck

Bedroom 3
12'-10" x 15'-2"
8'-8" Clg.

Open to Below
19'-8" to 20'-0"
Coffered Clg.

Guest Suite
11'-2" x 19'-8"
8'-8" Clg.

Walk-In Shower

Bath 3

Bath 2

Walk-In Shower

WIC

WIC

Attic Access

Balcony
8'-8" Clg.

Plant Shelf

Bedroom 2
12'-6" x 12'-10"
10'-8" Clg.

Open to Below

Balcony

LEVEL ONE

Veranda
12'-6" Clg.

Leisure Room
20'-8" x 39'-1"
11'-0" to 12'-0"
Coffered Clg.

Nook
9'-6" x 10'-0"
Stepped Clg.

Kitchen
13'-2" x 20'-0"
9'-6" to 10'-0"
Stepped Clg.

Veranda
20'-0" Clg.

Master Suite
14'-10" x 20'-6"
12'-0" to 10'-8"
Stepped Clg.

Pass-Thru

Utility
10'-0" Clg.

Living Room
16'-0" x 14'-4"
Open to Above

2 Sided Fireplace

Study
11'-2" x 12'-8"
10'-0" Clg.

WIC

WIC

Pantry

Art Niche

Gallery
10'-0" Clg.

Bench

Powder Bath

Dining
12'-10" x 13'-0"
10'-0" Clg.

Grand Foyer
Open to Above

Walk-In Shower

Garage
21'-2" x 34'-10"
10'-0" clg.

Entry
10'-10" Clg.

Master Bath
10'-0" Clg.

Whirlpool

©THE SATER DESIGN COLLECTION, INC.

Italian | **8003**

VILLA

ALESSANDRA

Massive square columns frame a spectacular portico and pedimented window above the entry of this romantic villa. Well-defined formal rooms offer both intimacy and grandeur, while the casual zone provides a lose-the-shoes atmosphere. Defined by a series of sculpted arches, the central corridor extends the plan's sight lines to the leisure and the master wings. On the upper level, a balcony hall connects three guest quarters that boast private decks.

Bed: **4**   Bath: **3-1/2**

Width: **85'0"**   Depth: **76'2"**

Level One: **2829** sq ft

Level Two: **1127** sq ft

Living Area: **3956** sq ft

Exterior Wall: **2x6**

Foundation: slab or optional basement

BEST LIVABILITY DESIGN AWARD

SATER DESIGN PLAN

See price index pages 186-187

WWW.EUROPEANHOUSEPLANS.COM © THE SATER DESIGN COLLECTION, INC.

REAR VIEW

Italian | 8007

VILLA

DELLA PORTA

Triple arches and stately columns grace the entry of this spacious Italian villa. Designed for 21st-century living, the interior plan creates flexible spaces that are not formal or self-conscious, but simply comfortable. Defined by arches, columns and magnificent views that extend beyond the veranda, the living room opens to the dining room and shares a two-sided fireplace with the study. Gatherings large and small may spill out onto the veranda— where an outdoor kitchen facilitates meals alfresco.

Bed: **3**   Bath: **3-1/2**

Width: **106'4"**   Depth: **102'4"**

Level One: **3654** sq ft

Living Area: **3654** sq ft

Exterior Wall: **2x6**

Foundation: slab, optional basement or optional walkout

SUPERB OUTDOOR · LIVING DESIGN

SATER DESIGN PLAN

See price index pages 186-187

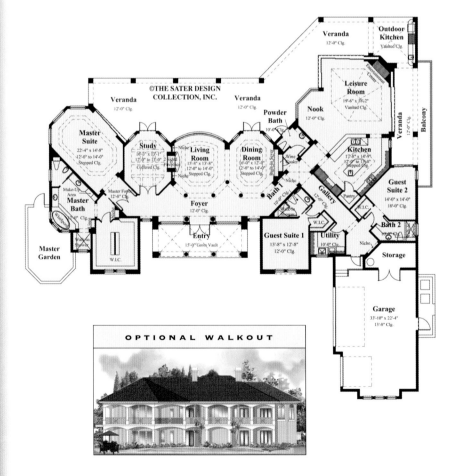

OPTIONAL WALKOUT

REAR VIEW

© THE SATER DESIGN COLLECTION, INC.

LEVEL ONE

LEVEL TWO

Italian | **8010**

VILLA RUSTICA

CAPUCINA

Stone gables complement the sculpted entry of this romantic, Italian country manor. An open arrangement of the gallery, formal living and dining rooms permits views of the rear through a two-story bow window. French doors open the leisure room to the outdoors, while the nook grants access to a lanai shared with the master suite's sitting bay. Upstairs, a balcony hall overlooking the living room connects the family bedrooms.

Bed: **4**   Bath: **4-1/2**

Width: **71'6"**   Depth: **83'0"**

Level One: **2855** sq ft

Level Two: **1156** sq ft

Living Area: **4011** sq ft

Bonus Room: **371** sq ft

Exterior Wall: **2x6**

Foundation: slab or optional basement

SATER DESIGN PLAN

See price index pages 186-187

REAR VIEW

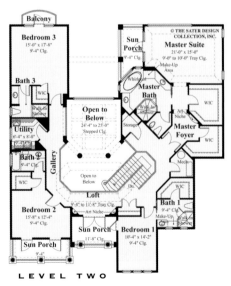

Italian | **8033**

ROCOCO

ISABELLA

Rococo elements frame the double portico, lending contrast to rugged stone accents and a rusticated stucco façade. The paneled entry leads to a two-story foyer that opens to the formal rooms. Private zones frame the rear loggias—a guest suite and the leisure room both open to the outdoor space. On the upper level, a loft overlooks the living room and accesses a sun porch. To the right, a foyer leads to the private master retreat.

Bed: **5**   Bath: **5-1/2**

Width: **58'0"**   Depth: **65'0"**

Level One: **2163** sq ft

Level Two: **2302** sq ft

Living Area: **4465** sq ft

Exterior Wall: **2x6**

Foundation: slab or optional basement

SATER DESIGN PLAN

See price index pages 186-187

LEVEL ONE

LEVEL TWO

REAR VIEW

© THE SATER DESIGN COLLECTION, INC.

WWW.EUROPEANHOUSEPLANS.COM

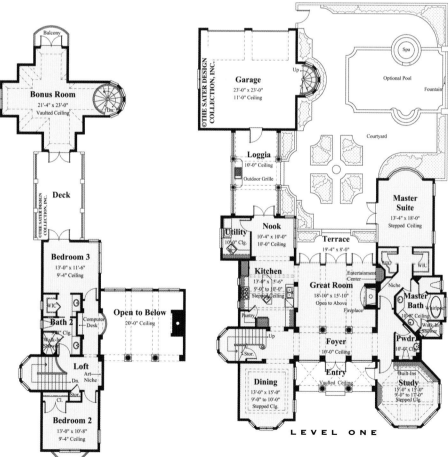

LEVEL TWO

LEVEL ONE

© THE SATER DESIGN COLLECTION, INC.

Italian | 8022

RENAISSANCE

BARTOLINI

Trefoil windows and a deeply sculpted portico set off a lyrical Italian aesthetic inspired by 15th-century forms and an oceanfront attitude. Inside, three sets of French doors open the great room to the courtyard and terrace. A private wing, that includes the kitchen and morning nook, also opens to the outdoors. The master suite enjoys ample amounts of space and privacy. The upper level harbors two guest suites, a loft and bonus room with a bay tower.

Bed: **3**   Bath: **2-1/2**

Width: **60'6"**   Depth: **94'0"**

Level One: **2084** sq ft

Level Two: **652** sq ft

Living Area: **2736** sq ft

Bonus Room: **375** sq ft

Exterior Wall: **2x6**

Foundation: slab or optional basement

SATER DESIGN PLAN

See price index pages 186-187

WWW.EUROPEANHOUSEPLANS.COM © THE SATER DESIGN COLLECTION, INC.

REAR VIEW

Italian | 8043

RENAISSANCE

SALINA

Hipped rooflines, carved eave brackets and varied gables evoke a sense of the past, while a blend of old and new prevails inside. Beamed and coffered ceilings juxtapose state-of-the-art amenities—a pass-thru wet bar, cutting-edge appliances in the kitchen, and a standalone media center between the leisure and game rooms. Rounded arches define the transitions between well-appointed rooms and open spaces. Near the rear of the plan, guest quarters and the leisure room open to the veranda and outdoor grille.

Bed: **4**   Bath: **3-1/2**

Width: **80'0"**   Depth: **104'8"**

Level One: **3743** sq ft

Living Area: **3743** sq ft

Exterior Wall: **2x6**

Foundation: slab or optional basement

SATER DESIGN PLAN

See price index pages 186-187

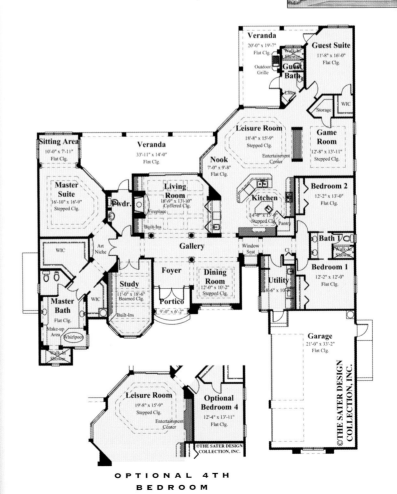

OPTIONAL 4TH BEDROOM

REAR VIEW

© THE SATER DESIGN COLLECTION, INC.

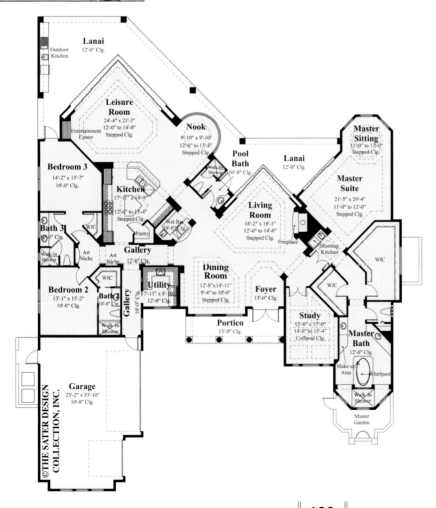

© THE SATER DESIGN COLLECTION, INC.

Italian | 8035

RENAISSANCE

LAPARELLI

Romantic elements reside throughout this Italian villa, melding style and views with a profound level of comfort. Arch-topped windows bring light into the forward formal spaces, while retreating glass walls along the rear extend both public and private realms outside. The kitchen serves the formal dining room via a gallery, while a wet bar announces the casual living space. The owners' retreat provides a magnificent bedroom with a morning kitchen and access to the wraparound lanai.

Bed: **3** Bath: **4**

Width: **83'10"** Depth: **106'0"**

Level One: **3942** sq ft

Living Area: **3942** sq ft

Exterior Wall: **2x6**

Foundation: slab

SATER DESIGN PLAN

See price index pages 186-187

133

REAR VIEW

WWW.EUROPEANHOUSEPLANS.COM   © THE SATER DESIGN COLLECTION, INC.

Italian | 8037

VILLA

RAPHAELLO

Turrets integrate the layered elevation, which draws its inspiration from 16th-century forms with symmetry, brackets and pilasters. New-World allocations of space defy tradition throughout the interior, creating a natural flow. Living spaces oriented to the rear of the plan take in expansive views through retreating glass walls and access the lanai. On the upper level, guest bedrooms open to a shared deck and a computer loft leads to a spacious bonus room.

Bed: **3** Bath: **3-1/2**

Width: **72'0"** Depth: **68'3"**

Level One: **2250** sq ft

Level Two: **663** sq ft

Living Area: **2913** sq ft

Bonus Room: **351** sq ft

Exterior Wall: **2x6**

Foundation: slab

SATER DESIGN PLAN

See price index pages 186-187

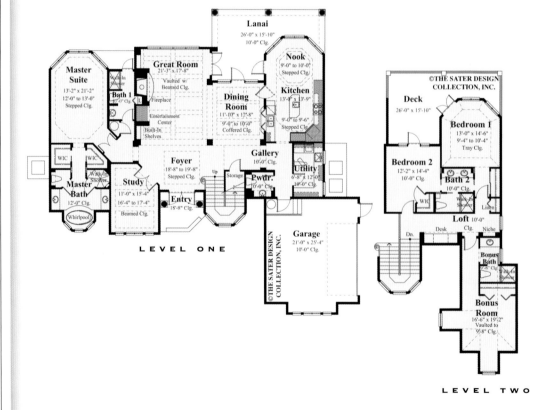

LEVEL ONE

LEVEL TWO

REAR VIEW

© THE SATER DESIGN COLLECTION, INC.

WWW.EUROPEANHOUSEPLANS.COM

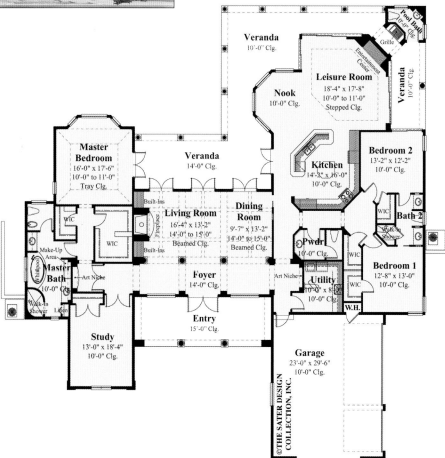

Veranda
10'-0" Clg.

Pool Bath
10'-0" Clg.

Grille

Entertainment Center

Leisure Room
18'-4" x 17'-8"
10'-0" to 11'-0"
Stepped Clg.

Nook
10'-0" Clg.

Veranda
10'-0" Clg.

Kitchen
14'-2" x 16'-0"
10'-0" Clg.

Bedroom 2
13'-2" x 12'-2"
10'-0" Clg.

Master Bedroom
16'-0" x 17'-6"
10'-0" to 11'-0"
Tray Clg.

Veranda
14'-0" Clg.

Built-Ins

WIC

Living Room
16'-4" x 13'-2"
14'-0" to 15'-0"
Beamed Clg.

Fireplace

WIC

Dining Room
9'-7" x 13'-2"
14'-0" to 15'-0"
Beamed Clg.

Built-Ins

WIC

Bath 2

Walk-In Shower

Make-Up Area

Master Bath
10'-0" Clg.

Whirlpool

Art Niche

Linen

Walk-In Shower

Foyer
14'-0" Clg.

Art Niche

Pwdr
10'-0" Clg.

Utility
10'-0" x 8'
10'-0" Clg.

WIC

WIC

Bedroom 1
12'-8" x 13'-0"
10'-0" Clg.

W.H.

Entry
15'-0" Clg.

Study
13'-0" x 18'-4"
10'-0" Clg.

Garage
23'-0" x 29'-6"
10'-0" Clg.

©THE SATER DESIGN COLLECTION, INC.

© THE SATER DESIGN COLLECTION, INC.

Italian | 8042

RENAISSANCE

BELLINI

Classic architectural lines surround an entry portico inspired by Italian villas. Ancient and modern elements come together throughout the interior, juxtaposing rusticated beamed ceilings with up-to-the-minute electronics. An open gallery announces the living/dining room—a space anchored by a massive fireplace. A state-of-the-art kitchen overlooks the nook and leisure room. Retreating glass walls open the space to a wraparound veranda that includes an outdoor grille and a secluded area for meals alfresco.

Bed: **3**   Bath: **2** Full & **2** Half

Width: **84'0"**   Depth: **92'2"**

Level One: **3351** sq ft

Living Area: **3351** sq ft

Exterior Wall: **2x6**

Foundation: slab

SUPERB OUTDOOR LIVING DESIGN

SATER DESIGN PLAN

See price index pages 186-187

REAR VIEW

Italian | 8073

COURTYARD

MEZZINA

This unique villa features private family and guest spaces with open connections to a spacious courtyard area. Past the portico, the foyer opens up to views beyond the grand salon's French doors. To the left, the kitchen connects to the formal dining room through a butler's pantry. Nearby, the leisure room opens to the loggia and outdoor kitchen. A gallery leads to two secluded guest suites, while a detached guest suite provides even more privacy.

Bed: **4**   Bath: **4-1/2**

Width: **69'10"**   Depth: **120'4"**

Level One: **4175** sq ft

Living Area: **4175** sq ft

Exterior Wall: **8" CBS**

Foundation: slab

BEST 2-STORY PLAN DESIGN

SATER DESIGN PLAN

See price index pages 186-187

NOT AVAILABLE FOR CONSTRUCTION IN LEE OR COLLIER COUNTIES, FL

©THE SATER DESIGN COLLECTION, INC.

REAR VIEW

© THE SATER DESIGN COLLECTION, INC.

WWW.EUROPEANHOUSEPLANS.COM

LEVEL TWO

WIC
Balcony
Flat Clg.
Balcony
Flat Clg.

Bedroom 3
14'-11" x 16'-0"
Flat Clg.

Open to
Below

Bedroom 4
13'-0" x 14'-6"
Flat Clg.

Walk-In
Shower

Walk-In
Shower

Bath 3

©THE SATER DESIGN
COLLECTION, INC.

Bath 4

WIC

WIC

Loft

Niche

Bedroom 2
14'-8" x 16'-4"
Flat Clg.

Balcony

LEVEL ONE

Veranda
Flat Clg.

Leisure
Room
17'-4" x 25'-2"
Tray Clg.

Nook
11'-9" x 9-2"
Stepped Clg.

Veranda
Flat Clg.
Pass-Thru

Veranda
Flat Clg.

Master
Suite
17'-0" x 23'-0"
Stepped Clg.

Kitchen
16'-4" x 21'-8"
Flat

Living Room
18'-2" x 19'-2"
Open to Above

Study
11'-8" x 14'-6"
Flat Clg.

Utility
11'-6" x 8'-0"

Gallery

Pantry

2-Sided
Fireplace

Built-Ins

WIC

WIC

Niche

Window Seat

Garage
22'-4" x 36'-8"
Flat Clg.

Pwdr.

Dining Room
14'-8" x 16'-4"
Flat Clg.

Foyer

Up

Dn.
Cl.

Walk-In
Shower

Portico

Master
Bath
Vaulted Clg.

Whirlpool

© THE SATER DESIGN
COLLECTION, INC.

|| 137 ||

Italian | 6765

RENAISSANCE

FLAGSTONE RIDGE

The dramatic use of stacked stone amidst arch-top windows gives this home a dignified and warm façade. A front portico under triple arches leads to the foyer and living room, where three pairs of French doors open to the veranda and breathtaking views. French doors also lead outside from the study, master suite and oversized leisure room. A second-floor loft views the living room and connects to three upstairs bedrooms.

Bed: **4**   Bath: **4-1/2**

Width: **95'0"**   Depth: **84'8"**

Level One: **3556** sq ft

Level Two: **1253** sq ft

Living Area: **4809** sq ft

Exterior Wall: **2x6**

Foundation: slab

BEST 2-STORY PLAN DESIGN

SATER RESERVE PLAN

Call for pricing

© THE SATER DESIGN COLLECTION, INC.

8034 WINTHROP

French

A confident, dignified sense of classic beauty melds seamlessly with state-of-the-art interiors in these award-winning designs. Grand turrets suggest both the permanence of a castle and exude the warmth of a welcoming family home. Elegant balconies, palatial columns and spectacular porticos announce two-story foyers, spacious formal rooms and flexible living spaces. Sunlight streams through open kitchens, verandahs and unparalleled master suites, while views extend through romantic archways and open French doors. Awash in extravagant details, such as art niches, built-ins, pocket doors and double-sided fireplaces, these homes evoke the true beauty, romance and splendor of France.

REAR VIEW

© THE SATER DESIGN COLLECTION, INC.

© THE SATER DESIGN COLLECTION, INC.

LEVEL TWO

LEVEL ONE

© THE SATER DESIGN COLLECTION, INC.

French | 8001

CHATEAUESQUE

ROYAL COUNTRY DOWN

Renaissance details—carved pilasters, rusticated columns and scrolled pediments-highlight the refined spirit of the home, which prevails beyond the grand entry. Formal spaces radiate from a gallery of arches and columns—a deliberate strategy that permits interior vistas past the rear veranda. Built-in shelves frame the fireplace in the leisure room, and anchor an open arrangement of casual space with the nook and kitchen. A spiral staircase leads to the guest quarters on the upper level.

Bed: **4**   Bath: **3-1/2**

Width: **85'0"**   Depth: **76'8"**

Level One: **2829** sq ft

Level Two: **1127** sq ft

Living Area: **3956** sq ft

Exterior Wall: **2x6**

Foundation: slab or optional basement

INNOVATIVE DESIGN AWARD

SATER DESIGN PLAN

See price index pages 186-187

WWW.EUROPEANHOUSEPLANS.COM   © THE SATER DESIGN COLLECTION, INC.

REAR VIEW

French | 8039

COUNTRY

MEDORO

Stickwork, shutters and bay windows embellish a brick façade influenced by the historic cottages of rural France. The arrangement of interior spaces permits the center of the home to flex from private to public use. Beamed and coffered ceilings enrich the amenities shared by the great room and formal dining room: an entertainment center, built-in shelves and fireplace. French doors connect the main zones with the lanai. Upstairs, guest bedrooms share a spacious deck.

Bed: **3**   Bath: **3-1/2**

Width: **72'0"**   Depth: **68'3"**

Level One: **2250** sq ft

Level Two: **663** sq ft

Living Area: **2913** sq ft

Bonus Room: **351** sq ft

Exterior Wall: **2x6**

Foundation: slab

SATER DESIGN PLAN

See price index pages 186-187

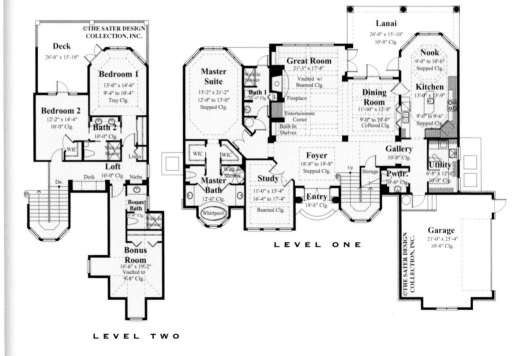

LEVEL TWO

LEVEL ONE

REAR VIEW

© THE SATER DESIGN COLLECTION, INC.

WWW.EUROPEANHOUSEPLANS.COM

Veranda
37'-2" x 12'-8"
12'-0" Clg.

Outdoor Grille

Built-Ins

Master Suite
14'-8" x 17'-0"
12'-0" to 13'-0"
Tray Clg.

WIC

Art Niche

Great Room
21'-0" x 17'-0"
Open to Above

Fireplace

Entertainment Center

Storage

Master Bath
11'-0" Clg.
Whirlpool

Walk-In Shower

Powder Bath

Study/Office
13'-0" x 13'-8"
9'-4" to 10'-0"
Beamed Clg.

Foyer
9'-4" to 10'-0"
Stepped Clg.

Dining
13'-0" x 12'-10"
9'-0" to 10'-0"
Stepped Clg.

Portico
10'-0" Clg.

Breakfast
13'-0" x 9'-0"
9'-4" to 10'-0"
Beamed Clg.

Kitchen
14'-6" x 10'-6"
9'-4" to 10'-0"
Beamed Clg.

Pantry
8'-8" Clg.

Utility
9'-0" x 6'-4"
9'-0" Clg.

Dn

Up

©THE SATER DESIGN COLLECTION, INC.

Garage
23'-0" x 24'-0"
10'-2" Clg.

LEVEL ONE

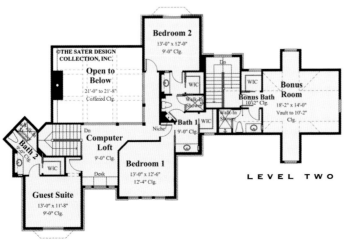

Bedroom 2
13'-0" x 12'-0"
9'-0" Clg.

©THE SATER DESIGN COLLECTION, INC.

Open to Below
21'-0" to 21'-8"
Coffered Clg.

WIC

Walk-In Shower

Bath 1
9'-0" Clg.

WIC

Niche

Bonus Bath
10'-2" Clg.

Walk-In Shower

Bonus Room
18'-2" x 14'-0"
Vault to 10'-2" Clg.

WIC

Bath 2

Dn

Computer Loft
9'-0" Clg.

Bedroom 1
13'-0" x 12'-6"
12'-4" Clg.

Desk

WIC

Guest Suite
13'-0" x 11'-8"
9'-0" Clg.

LEVEL TWO

French | **8005**

COUNTRY

CHANNING

State-of-the-art amenities reside together with a spirit of artisanship in this French country home. Inspired spaces flex from private to public, well-defined to wide open. Columns and arches articulate the foyer and formal dining room, yet allow the space to mingle with interior vistas granted by the great room. French doors expand the nook, great room and master suite to the veranda. Upstairs, a versatile computer loft connects three guest bedrooms.

Bed: **4**   Bath: **3-1/2**

Width: **91'0"**   Depth: **52'8"**

Level One: **2222** sq ft

Level Two: **1075** sq ft

Living Area: **3297** sq ft

Bonus Room: **405** sq ft

Exterior Wall: **2x6**

Foundation: slab

FAMILY-FRIENDLY LIVING DESIGN

SATER DESIGN PLAN

See price index pages 186-187

WWW.EUROPEANHOUSEPLANS.COM

© THE SATER DESIGN COLLECTION, INC.

REAR VIEW

French | 8009

NORMANDY

BAXTER

A stunning arcade, enhanced with fanlights and French doors, leads to a grand interior that is oriented to rear vistas. Retreating walls, glass doors, and bow and bay windows permit plenty of natural light and spectacular views to fill the home. Classic materials and a historic style play well against extraordinary touches, such as a two-way fireplace, stepped ceilings and an angled entertainment center in the leisure room and state-of-the-art appliances in the kitchen.

Bed: **3** Bath: **3-1/2**

Width: **106'4"** Depth: **102'4"**

Level One: **3652** sq ft

Living Area: **3652** sq ft

Exterior Wall: **2x6**

Foundation: slab, optional basement or optional walkout

VIEW·ORIENTED LIVING DESIGN

SATER DESIGN PLAN

See price index pages 186-187

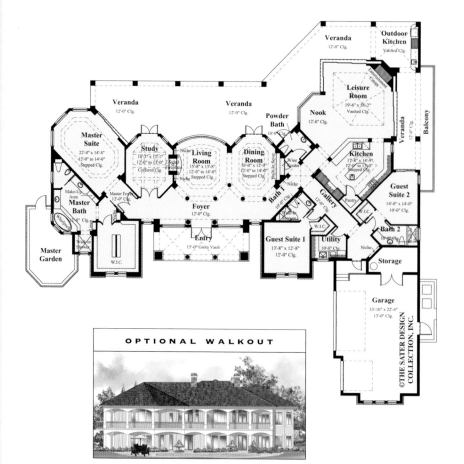

OPTIONAL WALKOUT

REAR VIEW

© THE SATER DESIGN COLLECTION, INC.

WWW.EUROPEANHOUSEPLANS.COM

French | 8011

NORMANDY

LA RIVIERE

Arched windows and dormers set off a rich blend of clapboard, stucco and stone with this New-World villa. An open arrangement of the public zone secures panoramic views within each of the formal spaces. The living room boasts a sense of nature granted through a two-story bow window, framed by bay windows in the nook and master suite. On the upper level, a computer loft links the guest bedrooms and a step-down bonus room.

Bed: **4** Bath: **4-1/2**

Width: **71'6"** Depth: **83'0"**

Level One: **2849** sq ft

Level Two: **1156** sq ft

Living Area: **4005** sq ft

Bonus Room: **371** sq ft

Exterior Wall: **2x6**

Foundation: slab or optional basement

SATER DESIGN PLAN

See price index pages 186-187

LEVEL ONE

LEVEL TWO

© THE SATER DESIGN COLLECTION, INC.

WWW.EUROPEANHOUSEPLANS.COM   © THE SATER DESIGN COLLECTION, INC.

REAR VIEW

French | 8015

COUNTRY

BURKE HOUSE

Simply beautiful, this French Country manor promises 21st-century repose combined with Old-World architecture. A two-story coffered ceiling plays counterpoint to a two-sided fireplace shared by the living room and study. Walls of glass define the rear perimeter, permitting views throughout the home. The kitchen adjoins a wet bar leading to the formal dining room. Upstairs, two lofts connect three guest bedrooms and a bonus room.

Bed: **4**   Bath: **4-1/2**

Width: **70'0"**   Depth: **100'0"**

Level One: **3023** sq ft

Level Two: **1623** sq ft

Living Area: **4646** sq ft

Bonus Room: **294** sq ft

Exterior Wall: **2x6**

Foundation: slab or optional basement

SATER DESIGN PLAN

See price index pages 186-187

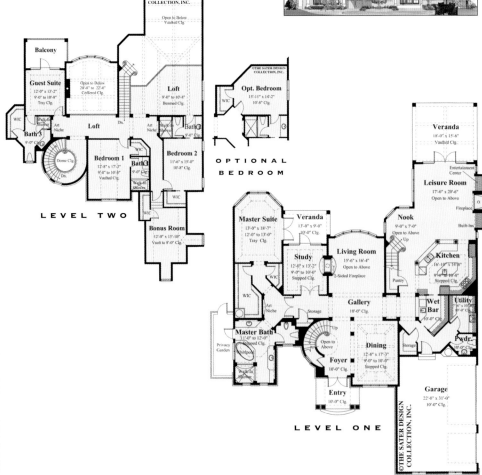

LEVEL TWO

OPTIONAL BEDROOM

LEVEL ONE

REAR VIEW

© THE SATER DESIGN COLLECTION, INC.   WWW.EUROPEANHOUSEPLANS.COM

©THE SATER DESIGN COLLECTION, INC.

Garage
25'-0" x 23'-0"
8'-8" Clg.

Outdoor Grille   10'-0" Clg.

Veranda
40'-8" x 14'-0"
Open to Above

Nook
10'-8" x 8'-8"
9'-4" to 10'-0"
Stepped Clg.

Computer Center
10'-0" Clg.

Art Niche

Utility
9'-4" x 9'-6"
10'-0" Clg.

Kitchen
13'-6" x 13'-6"
9'-4" to 10'-0"
Stepped Clg.

Leisure Room
15'-8" x 19'-8"
Open to Above

Entertainment Center

2-Sided Fireplace

Study
11'-4" x 15'-0"
13'-4" to 14'-0"
Beamed Clg.

Built-Ins

Morning Kitchen

Master Suite
12'-6" x 18'-6"
13'-8" Tray Clg.

WIC

Stair Tower
Sitting Alcove

Art Niche

Gallery
10'-0" Clg.

Master Foyer

Make-Up Area

Walk-In Shelves

Dining Room
13'-0" x 13'-0"
9'-4" to 10'-0"
Stepped Clg.

Powder Bath

Foyer
Open to Above

Living Room
13'-0" x 13'-0"
9'-4" to 10'-0"
Coffered Clg.

Master Bath
11'-0" Clg.

Whirlpool

Linen

Portico
36'-0" x 8'-0"
10'-0" Clg.

LEVEL ONE

©THE SATER DESIGN COLLECTION, INC.

Bonus Room
25'-0" x 14'-8"
Vaulted Clg.

Sun Porch
9'-4" Clg.

Bedroom 2
15'-4" x 14'-6"
10'-8" Clg.

Bath 1
10'-0" Clg.

WIC

Storage

Open to Below
22'-0" to 23'-0"
Stepped Clg.

Loft
10'-8" Clg.
Dn

Computer Desk

Built-In Shelves

Balcony
10'-0" Clg.

Art Niche

Guest Bath
10'-0" Clg.

Attic Space

WIC

WIC

Bedroom 1
13'-0" x 11'-10"
10'-8" Clg.

Open to Below
22'-0" to 23'-0"
Stepped Clg.

Guest Suite
13'-0" x 13'-2"
10'-8" Clg.

Porch
36'-0" x 8'-0"
9'-4" Clg.

LEVEL TWO

© THE SATER DESIGN COLLECTION, INC.

French | 8017

REVIVAL

LES TOURELLES

A steeply pitched roof caps porticos reminiscent of the early French houses of the southeastern coastal regions, while a thoughtfully placed turret reinvents traffic flow within. Formal rooms flank the foyer and open to the gallery. At the center of the plan, great views dominate the two-story leisure room, which leads out to the veranda. Past the study, double doors open to the master suite. On the upper level, three guest bedrooms enjoy deck access.

Bed: **4**   Bath: **3-1/2**

Width: **83'0"**   Depth: **71'8"**

Level One: **2481** sq ft

Level Two: **1132** sq ft

Living Area: **3613** sq ft

Bonus Room: **332** sq ft

Exterior Wall: **2x6**

Foundation: slab or optional basement

BEST 2-STORY PLAN DESIGN

SATER DESIGN PLAN

See price index pages 186-187

REAR VIEW

WWW.EUROPEANHOUSEPLANS.COM © THE SATER DESIGN COLLECTION, INC.

French | 8018

CHATEAUX

BELLAMY

Well-crafted millwork, pediments and dormers reinforce a Chateauesque theme with this vernacular design. Transoms and fanlights extend the motif outside and lend natural light to the interior. A sense of French tradition is reiterated in the public realm with an enfilade arrangement of rooms—the living and dining rooms opposite the leisure room and study. A spiral staircase employs the turret to bring light to the main and upper galleries.

Bed: **4**   Bath: **3-1/2**

Width: **83'0"**   Depth: **71'8"**

Level One: **2483** sq ft

Level Two: **1127** sq ft

Living Area: **3610** sq ft

Bonus Room: **332** sq ft

Exterior Wall: **2x6**

Foundation: slab or optional basement

SATER DESIGN PLAN

See price index pages 186-187

LEVEL ONE

LEVEL TWO

REAR VIEW

© THE SATER DESIGN COLLECTION, INC.

WWW.EUROPEANHOUSEPLANS.COM

LEVEL ONE

©THE SATER DESIGN COLLECTION, INC.

Veranda
10'-0" x 18'-6"
10'-8" Clg.

Garage
25'-0" x 22'-0"
12'-0" Clg.

Outdoor Kitchen

Veranda
34'-0" x 13'-8"
14'-8" Clg.

Nook
13'-0" x 10'-10"
10'-0" to 10'-8" Stepped Clg.

Mud Room
7'-8" x 8'-4"
10'-8" Clg.

Master Suite
13'-0" x 16'-10"
10'-8" to 12'-8" Stepped Clg.

Great Room
19'-6" x 15'-3"
Open to Above

Built-Ins

Fireplace

Built-Ins

WIC

Kitchen
13'-6" x 13'-4"
10'-0" to 10'-8" Stepped Clg.

Utility
8' x 7'-5"
10'-8" Clg.

Master Foyer

WIC

Pantry

Pwdr

Master Bath
10'-8" Clg.

Art Niche

Gallery
10'-8" Clg.

Up

Whirlpool   Walk-In Shower

Foyer
10'-8" Clg.

Friends' Entry
10'-8" Clg.

Study
13'-0" x 14'-2"
10'-0" to 10'-8" Stepped Clg.

Portico
10'-8" Clg.

Dining Room
13'-0" x 13'-10"
10'-2" to 10'-8" Coffered Clg.

LEVEL TWO

Guest Deck
10'-0" x 18'-6"

Open to Below
21'-4" to 22'-0"
Coffered Clg.

Guest Suite
19'-2" x 13'-0"
9'-0" to 10'-0" Tray Clg.

Built-In

Walk-In Shower

Stor.
9'-4" Clg.

©THE SATER DESIGN COLLECTION, INC.

W.I.C.

Guest Bath

Walk-In Shower

Bath 2

WIC

Loft
9'-4" x 10'-0"
Stepped Clg.

Built-In Dn
Bookshelves

Built-In Desk

Bath 1
9'-4" Clg.

Bedroom 2
13'-0" x 13'-10"
12'-4" Clg.

Sun Porch
9'-4" Clg.

Bedroom 1
13'-0" x 13'-0"
9'-4" Clg.

French | 8021

NEO-CLASSIC

NEW BRUNSWICK

Symmetry surrounds a double portico on a distinctly American façade that's rooted in a rich European past. A grand foyer opens to the perfect balance of well-defined formal rooms and inviting casual spaces. The prevalent use of natural light is a primary objective in the design—French doors and bay windows surround the main-level plan, while well-placed windows and access to outdoor places brighten the upper level. A convenient friends entry leads to the upstairs bedrooms.

Bed: **4**   Bath: **4-1/2**

Width: **80'0"**   Depth: **63'9"**

Level One: **2232** sq ft

Level Two: **1269** sq ft

Living Area: **3501** sq ft

Exterior Wall: **2x6**

Foundation: slab or optional basement

BEST LIVABILITY DESIGN AWARD

SATER DESIGN PLAN

See price index pages 186-187

© THE SATER DESIGN COLLECTION, INC.

REAR VIEW

French | 8024

NORMANDY

GABRIEL

Arches and stone gables frame an airy arcade in this classic chateaux. The center doors lead to a gallery foyer and great room, anchored by a massive fireplace. French doors open the space to the courtyard. To the left of the plan, a loggia harbors an eating area, which can be accessed from the nook and kitchen. Upstairs, a loft overlooks the great room and links the guest suites. A rear deck leads to a versatile bonus room.

Bed: **3**   Bath: **2-1/2**

Width: **60'6"**   Depth: **94'0"**

Level One: **2084** sq ft

Level Two: **652** sq ft

Living Area: **2736** sq ft

Bonus Room: **365** sq ft

Exterior Wall: **2x6**

Foundation: slab or optional basement

SUPERB OUTDOOR LIVING DESIGN

SATER DESIGN PLAN

See price index pages 186-187

LEVEL ONE

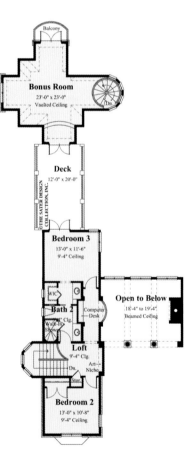

LEVEL TWO

© THE SATER DESIGN COLLECTION, INC.

WWW.EUROPEANHOUSEPLANS.COM

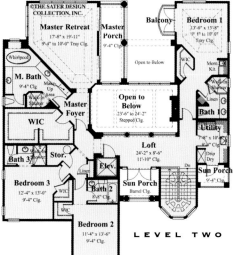

REAR VIEW

LEVEL ONE

LEVEL TWO

© THE SATER DESIGN COLLECTION, INC.

French | 8026

COUNTRY

SAINT-GERMAIN

Sculpted outdoor places lend definition to the elevation, reiterating a highly crafted interior. At the heart of the home, flexible public spaces take on an elegant formality for planned events, yet provide a comfortable retreat for everday use. Nearby, the library/study features double doors to the veranda. Upstairs, a wraparound loft overlooks the living space and links guest quarters to the owners' retreat. A convenient elevator complements the staircase, which winds upward from the foyer.

Bed: **5**   Bath: **5-1/2**

Width: **58'0"**   Depth: **65'0"**

Level One: **1996** sq ft

Level Two: **2171** sq ft

Living Area: **4167** sq ft

Exterior Wall: **2x6**

Foundation: slab or optional basement

SATER DESIGN PLAN

See price index pages 186-187

VIEW-ORIENTED LIVING DESIGN

REAR VIEW

WWW.EUROPEANHOUSEPLANS.COM   © THE SATER DESIGN COLLECTION, INC.

French | 8030

REVIVAL

KINSLEY

Natural textures of brick and stone play counterpoint to revival elements, suggesting a neoclassic influence in this French manor. Formal rooms grant a strong visual connection to the outdoors, with the exception of the study, which is secluded by pocket doors. A massive fireplace and beamed ceiling offer an authentic presence in the great room. Drawing on coastal vernaculars, the rear of the home opens to the veranda creating a seamless connection with the outdoors.

Bed: **3**   Bath: **2-1/2**

Width: **62'10"**   Depth: **73'6"**

Level One: **2191** sq ft

Living Area: **2191** sq ft

Exterior Wall: **2x6**

Foundation: slab or optional basement

SATER DESIGN PLAN

See price index pages 186-187

© THE SATER DESIGN COLLECTION, INC.

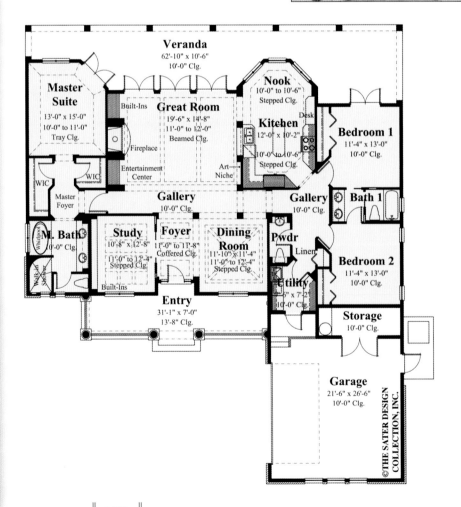

Veranda
62'-10" x 10'-6"
10'-0" Clg.

Master Suite
13'-0" x 15'-0"
10'-0" to 11'-0"
Tray Clg.

Built-Ins

Great Room
19'-6" x 14'-8"
11'-0" to 12'-0"
Beamed Clg.

Nook
10'-0" to 10'-6"
Stepped Clg.

Desk

Kitchen
12'-0" x 10'-2"

Bedroom 1
11'-4" x 13'-0"
10'-0" Clg.

Fireplace

10'-0" to 10'-6"
Stepped Clg.

Entertainment Center

Art Niche

WIC   WIC

Master Foyer

Gallery
10'-0" Clg.

Gallery
10'-0" Clg.

Bath 1

M. Bath
10'-0" Clg.

Whirlpool

Study
10'-8" x 12'-8"
11'-0" to 12'-4"
Stepped Clg.

Foyer
11'-0" to 11'-8"
Coffered Clg.

Dining Room
11'-10" x 11'-4"
11'-0" to 12'-4"
Stepped Clg.

Pwdr

Linen

Bedroom 2
11'-4" x 13'-0"
10'-0" Clg.

Walk-in Shower

Built-Ins

Utility
x 7'-2"
10'-0" Clg.

Entry
31'-1" x 7'-0"
13'-8" Clg.

Storage
10'-0" Clg.

Garage
21'-6" x 26'-6"
10'-0" Clg.

©THE SATER DESIGN COLLECTION, INC.

REAR VIEW

© THE SATER DESIGN COLLECTION, INC.

WWW.EUROPEANHOUSEPLANS.COM

LEVEL ONE

LEVEL TWO

French | 8032

BEAUX ARTS

STONEHAVEN

Cornice-line brackets and a triple-arch entry set off a grand plan with a host of windows and outdoor living areas. The foyer opens to the heart of the interior— an expansive center of formal and informal rooms, defined only by decorative columns and ceiling treatments. Views and natural light fill the home through a wall of glass to the rear of the plan. Upstairs, a wrap-around loft connects the master retreat with three guest suites.

Bed: **5**   Bath: **5-1/2**

Width: **58'0"**   Depth: **65'0"**

Level One: **2163** sq ft

Level Two: **2302** sq ft

Living Area: **4465** sq ft

Exterior Wall: **2x6**

Foundation: slab or optional basement

SATER DESIGN PLAN

See price index pages 186-187

REAR VIEW

French | 8060

NORMANDY

LE MARESCOTT

A flared eave sets a very French tone for this neo-Norman façade. An interior of intimate spaces, angled walls and open rooms melds state-of-the-art technology with a sense of nature. Retreating glass doors expand the living and leisure rooms to the lanai. The kitchen is centrally located between the formal and informal realms, making entertaining easy. The generous master retreat enjoys privacy away from three guest bedroooms on the opposite side of the home.

Bed: **4**   Bath: **3-1/2**

Width: **67'0"**   Depth: **90'8"**

Level One: **3246** sq ft

Living Area: **3246** sq ft

Exterior Wall: **2x6**

Foundation: slab

SATER DESIGN PLAN

See price index pages 186-187

REAR VIEW

© THE SATER DESIGN COLLECTION, INC.

WWW.EUROPEANHOUSEPLANS.COM

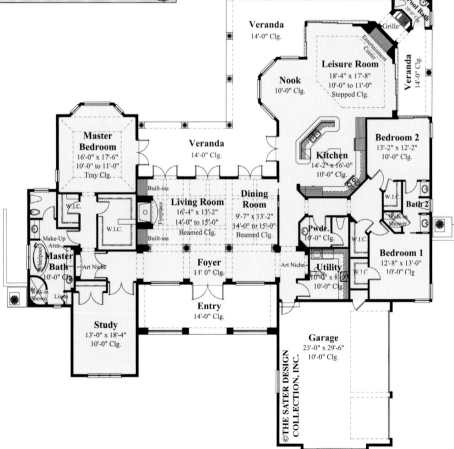

Veranda
14'-0" Clg.

Pool Bath
10'-0" Clg.

Grille

Leisure Room
18'-4" x 17'-8"
10'-0" to 11'-0"
Stepped Clg.

Nook
10'-0" Clg.

Veranda
14'-0" Clg.

Kitchen
14'-2" x 16'-0"
10'-0" Clg.

Bedroom 2
13'-2" x 12'-2"
10'-0" Clg.

Master
Bedroom
16'-0" x 17'-6"
10'-0" to 11'-0"
Tray Clg.

Veranda
14'-0" Clg.

Bath 2
Walk-in
Shower

W.I.C.

Built-ins

Living Room
16'-4" x 13'-2"
14'-0" to 15'-0"
Beamed Clg.

Dining
Room
9'-7" x 13'-2"
14'-0" to 15'-0"
Beamed Clg.

Built-ins

Fireplace

Make-Up
Area

Whirlpool

Master
Bath
10'-0" Clg.

Walk-in
Shower

Linen

Art Niche

Foyer
14' 0" Clg.

Pwdr.
10'-0" Clg.

Art Niche

Utility
10'-0" x 8'-0"
10'-0" Clg.

Bedroom 1
12'-8" x 13'-0"
10'-0" Clg.

W.I.C.

Entry
14'-0" Clg.

Study
13'-0" x 18'-4"
10'-0" Clg.

Garage
23'-0" x 29'-6"
10'-0" Clg.

© THE SATER DESIGN COLLECTION, INC.

French | 8040

RENAISSANCE

BRITTANY

This enchanting villa is more than a home—it's a lifestyle. Centered formal spaces cater to large parties yet easily convert to an intimate gathering spot. French doors extend the living area to the wraparound veranda, which boasts a cabana-style bath and outdoor grille. Away from the public realm, the master retreat enjoys access to the study. On the opposite side of the home, a hall links guest suites with the casual living area and kitchen.

Bed: **3**   Bath: **2** Full & **2** Half

Width: **84'0"**   Depth: **92'0"**

Level One: **3353** sq ft

Living Area: **3353** sq ft

Exterior Wall: **2x6**

Foundation: slab

SUPERB OUTDOOR LIVING DESIGN

SATER DESIGN PLAN

See price index pages 186-187

WWW.EUROPEANHOUSEPLANS.COM © THE SATER DESIGN COLLECTION, INC.

REAR VIEW

French | 8044

RENAISSANCE

BEAUCHAMP

Rusticated pilasters, pediments and quoins set off a symmetrical façade that calls up the aristocratic lines of 16th-century French villas. Past the gallery hall a pass-thru wet bar connects the formal living room with the kitchen, ensuring easy entertaining. An island entertainment center provides definition to the casual zone, separating the game room and the leisure space, which opens to the outdoors. Tucked away on the opposite side of the home, the master suite offers repose.

Bed: **4** Bath: **3-1/2**

Width: **80'8"** Depth: **104'8"**

Level One: **3790** sq ft

Living Area: **3790** sq ft

Exterior Wall: **2x6**

Foundation: slab or optional basement

SATER DESIGN PLAN

See price index pages 186-187

OPTIONAL 3RD BEDROOM

REAR VIEW

© THE SATER DESIGN COLLECTION, INC.

WWW.EUROPEANHOUSEPLANS.COM

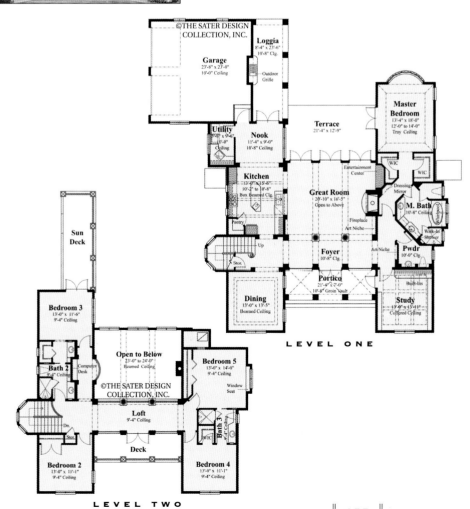

LEVEL ONE

LEVEL TWO

© THE SATER DESIGN COLLECTION, INC.

French | 8051

NEO-CLASSIC

SOLAINE

Rusticated columns and the balcony balustrade on this stately elevation suggest early 20th-century influences, yet the interior is purely modern. Well-defined formal rooms flank the gallery leading to the great room. Three sets of French doors link the space to the terrace. Nearby, a loggia boasts an outdoor grille and access to the nook and kitchen. The right wing of the home is dedicated to the owners' retreat. Upstairs, a gallery loft connects four guest bedrooms.

Bed: **5**   Bath: **3-1/2**
Width: **71'0"**   Depth: **72'0"**
Level One: **2163** sq ft
Level Two: **1415** sq ft
Living Area: **3578** sq ft
Exterior Wall: **2x6**
Foundation: slab

SATER DESIGN PLAN

See price index pages 186-187

WWW.EUROPEANHOUSEPLANS.COM   © THE SATER DESIGN COLLECTION, INC.

REAR VIEW

French | 8053

COUNTRY

CHRISTABEL

Stacked stone and wood shutters lend rural elements to this urbane design. The spacious interior offers open-air vistas from every room of the house. A refined arrangement of the forward rooms plays counterpoint to the state-of-the-art casual zone, which boasts a wall-sized entertainment center. For easy entertaining, the wet bar acts as a pass-thru from the kitchen to the dining room. Retreating walls grant access to the lanai and courtyard warmed by a fireplace.

Bed: **4**   Bath: **3-1/2**

Width: **74'8"**   Depth: **118'0"**

Level One: **2974** sq ft

Bonus Room: **297** sq ft

Living Area: **3271** sq ft

Exterior Wall: **2x6**

Foundation: slab

SATER DESIGN PLAN

See price index pages 186-187

REAR VIEW

© THE SATER DESIGN COLLECTION, INC.

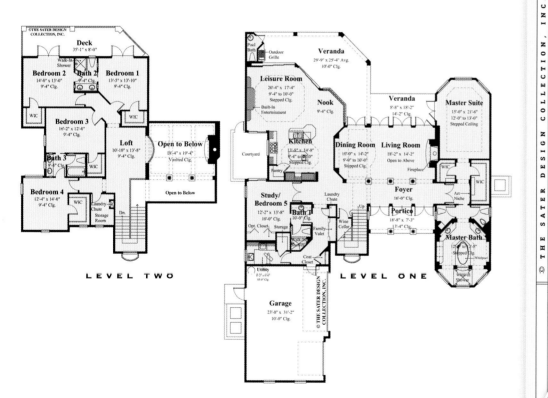

LEVEL TWO

LEVEL ONE

© THE SATER DESIGN COLLECTION, INC.

French | 8056

NORMANDY

ARGENTELLAS

Dormers and a graceful colonnade live in harmony with turrets and staggered rooflines on this modern elevation. Surprises prevail throughout the interior, with nature flowing into the formal rooms. A gallery foyer links two private wings and grants panoramic views through the rear of the plan. On the main level, the master wing offers a place of respite. Upstairs, four guest bedrooms and a loft are the perfect retreat for guests.

Bed: **6**   Bath: **4-1/2**

Width: **69'4"**   Depth: **95'4"**

Level One: **2920** sq ft

Level Two: **1478** sq ft

Living Area: **4398** sq ft

Exterior Wall:

8" CBS OR 2X6

Foundation: slab or optional basement

FAMILY-FRIENDLY LIVING DESIGN

SATER DESIGN PLAN

See price index pages 186-187

6932 MARTINIQUE

Spanish

An intoxicating mix of courtyards, arched loggias, turrets and porticos—these Spanish-inspired homes evoke a sense of timeless romanticism. Expansive verandahs, decks and balconies extend the living areas into the outdoors and welcome friends and family to gather, laugh and enjoy. Generous living rooms flow freely into formal dining areas. Gourmet-caliber kitchens open into breakfast nooks and leisure rooms—creating a common living space destined to become a favorite gathering area for friends and family. Bold and simply beautiful, these Mediterranean manors promise 21st-century repose combined with Old-World character and ambiance.

REAR VIEW

© THE SATER DESIGN COLLECTION, INC.

WWW.EUROPEANHOUSEPLANS.COM

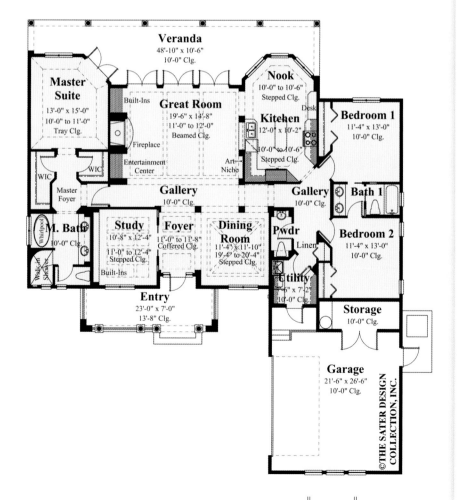

Veranda
48'-10" x 10'-6"
10'-0" Clg.

Master Suite
13'-0" x 15'-0"
10'-0" to 11'-0"
Tray Clg.

Great Room
19'-6" x 14'-8"
11'-0" to 12'-0"
Beamed Clg.

Built-Ins

Nook
10'-0" to 10'-6"
Stepped Clg.

Desk

Kitchen
12'-0" x 10'-2"
10'-0" to 10'-6"
Stepped Clg.

Bedroom 1
11'-4" x 13'-0"
10'-0" Clg.

Fireplace

Entertainment Center

WIC

WIC

Art Niche

Master Foyer

Gallery
10'-0" Clg.

Gallery
10'-0" Clg.

Bath 1

M. Bath
10'-0" Clg.

Study
10'-8" x 12'-4"
11'-0" to 12'-4"
Stepped Clg.

Foyer
11'-0" to 11'-8"
Coffered Clg.

Dining Room
11'-4" x 11'-10"
19'-4" to 20'-4"
Stepped Clg.

Pwdr

Linen

Bedroom 2
11'-4" x 13'-0"
10'-0" Clg.

Built-Ins

Utility
5'-6" x 7'-2"
10'-0" Clg.

Entry
23'-0" x 7'-0"
13'-8" Clg.

Storage
10'-0" Clg.

Garage
21'-6" x 26'-6"
10'-0" Clg.

©THE SATER DESIGN COLLECTION, INC.

© THE SATER DESIGN COLLECTION, INC.

Spanish | 8028

VILLA

MERCATO

Spiral columns articulate an elegant arcade that's merely the beginning of this Mediterranean villa. Inside, a beamed ceiling contributes a sense of spaciousness to the heart of the home, while walls of glass draw the outdoors inside. Varied ceiling treatments and sculpted arches define the wide-open interior, permitting flexibility as well as great views. The great room is anchored by a massive fireplace flanked by built-in shelves and an entertainment center—visible from the kitchen via a pass-thru.

Bed: **3**   Bath: **2-1/2**

Width: **62'10"**   Depth: **73'6"**

Level One: **2191** sq ft

Living Area: **2191** sq ft

Exterior Wall: **2x6**

Foundation: slab or optional basement

INNOVATIVE DESIGN AWARD

SATER DESIGN PLAN

See price index pages 186-187

www.europeanhouseplans.com © THE SATER DESIGN COLLECTION, INC.

REAR VIEW

Spanish | 8078

COURTYARD

TRE MORI

The classic façade is graced with low-pitched, projecting gables, Palladian-style windows and a triple-arch entry decorated with wrought-iron. Past the groin-vaulted entry, an enchanting courtyard greets visitors in this Spanish-inspired villa. Beyond the foyer, the kitchen flows into the nook and leisure room, extending onto the loggia through retreating glass doors. Secluded guest suites include the upstairs with its private balcony, and the first floor detached with pool view.

Bed: **5** Bath: **5-1/2**

Width: **69'10"** Depth: **120'0"**

Level One: **3683** sq ft

Level Two: **563** sq ft

Guest Suite: **310** sq ft

Living Area: **4556** sq ft

Exterior Wall: **8" CBS**

Foundation: slab

SATER DESIGN PLAN

See price index pages 186-187

LEVEL ONE

LEVEL TWO

NOT AVAILABLE FOR CONSTRUCTION IN LEE OR COLLIER COUNTIES, FL

© THE SATER DESIGN COLLECTION, INC.

REAR VIEW

NOT AVAILABLE FOR CONSTRUCTION
IN LEE OR COLLIER COUNTIES, FL

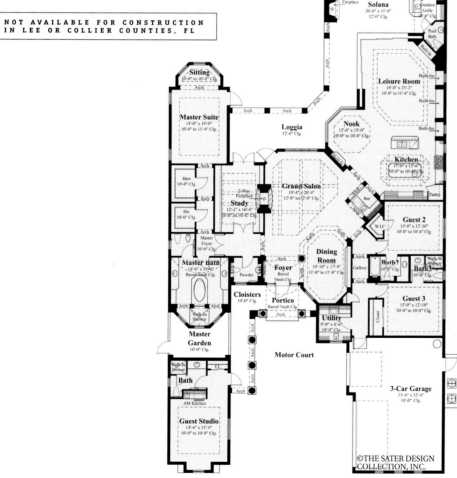

©THE SATER DESIGN COLLECTION, INC.

© THE SATER DESIGN COLLECTION, INC.

Spanish | 8074

ROCOCO REVIVAL

PALAZZO RIPOLI

Arches line the cloister flowing from the detached guest suite to the barrel-vault entry of this innovative design. Inside, the grand salon welcomes with commanding views past the loggia and a two-sided fireplace shared with the study. A walk-in wet bar adjoins the kitchen and provides a servery to the formal areas. Retreating glass walls open the leisure room to the outside amenities. To the left of the plan, the master wing is an indulgent retreat for the owners.

Bed: **4**   Bath: **4** Full, **2** Half

Width: **69'10"**   Depth: **120'0"**

Level One: **4266** sq ft

Living Area: **4266** sq ft

Exterior Wall: **8" CBS**

Foundation: slab

SATER DESIGN PLAN

See price index pages 186-187

WWW.EUROPEANHOUSEPLANS.COM © THE SATER DESIGN COLLECTION, INC.

REAR VIEW

Spanish | 8014

VILLA

SAN LORENZO

Revival elements—quoins, fractables and sculpted masonry surrounds—recall the beauty of rural Spanish villas. A coffered ceiling and a two-story bow window brighten the core of the plan—the living room—which shares a two-sided fireplace with the study. Nearby, a spiral stairway winds through the turret, linking with a balcony loft. An open arrangement of the leisure room and kitchen permits breezes to circulate through the entire wing.

Bed: **4**   Bath: **4-1/2**

Width: **70'0"**   Depth: **100'0"**

Level One: **3025** sq ft

Level Two: **1639** sq ft

Living Area: **4664** sq ft

Bonus Room: **294** sq ft

Exterior Wall: **2x6**

Foundation: slab or optional basement

SATER DESIGN PLAN

See price index pages 186-187

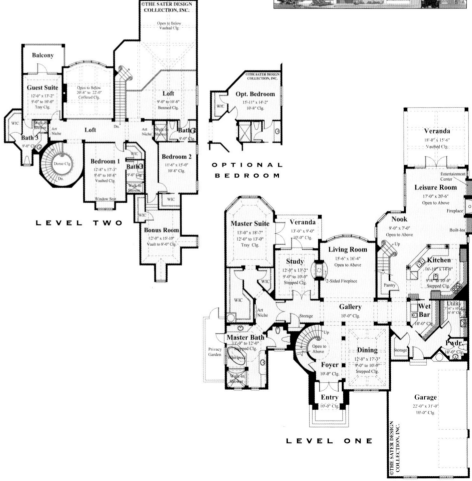

LEVEL TWO

OPTIONAL BEDROOM

LEVEL ONE

REAR VIEW

© THE SATER DESIGN COLLECTION, INC.

WWW.EUROPEANHOUSEPLANS.COM

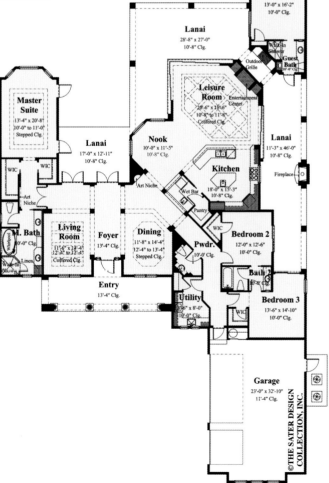

Guest Suite
13'-0" x 16'-2"
10'-0" Clg.

Lanai
28'-8" x 27'-0"
10'-8" Clg.

Master Suite
13'-4" x 20'-8"
10'-0" to 11'-0"
Stepped Clg.

Leisure Room
20'-6" x 18'-6"
10'-8" to 11'8"
Coffered Clg.

Lanai
17'-0" x 12'-11"
10'-8" Clg.

Nook
10'-0" x 11'-5"
10'-8" Clg.

Lanai
11'-3" x 46'-0"
10'-8" Clg.

Kitchen
18'-0" x 15'-3"
10'-8" Clg.

Fireplace

M. Bath
10'-0" Clg.

Living Room
11'-6" x 18'-4"
12'-9" to 13'-4"
Coffered Clg.

Foyer
13'-4" Clg.

Dining
11'-8" x 14'-4"
12'-4" to 13'-4"
Stepped Clg.

Pwdr.
10'-0" Clg.

Bedroom 2
12'-0" x 12'-6"
10'-0" Clg.

Entry
13'-4"

Utility
13'-6" x 8'-0"
10'-0" Clg.

Bath 2

Bedroom 3
13'-6" x 14'-10"
10'-0" Clg.

Garage
23'-0" x 32'-10"
11'-4" Clg.

©THE SATER DESIGN COLLECTION, INC.

© THE SATER DESIGN COLLECTION, INC.

Spanish | 8052

MOORISH

CAPRINA

Evocative of the adobe escapes of the Spanish Colonial vernacular, this exquisite villa intergrates the graceful interior with the outdoors. Paneled doors lead to a grand foyer, which defies convention with a no-walls approach to the formal rooms. Coffered ceilings provide spatial separation and a visual link between the public realms. Dramatic views further define the interior, and a wraparound lanai sends an invitation, to enjoy the outdoors.

Bed: **4**   Bath: **3-1/2**

Width: **74'8"**   Depth: **118'0"**

Level One: **2974** sq ft

Bonus Room: **297** sq ft

Living Area: **3271** sq ft

Exterior Wall: **2x6**

Foundation: slab

BEST 1-STORY PLAN DESIGN

SATER DESIGN PLAN

See price index pages 186-187

REAR VIEW

WWW.EUROPEANHOUSEPLANS.COM   © THE SATER DESIGN COLLECTION, INC.

Spanish | 8058
COLONIAL REVIVAL

PORTA ROSSA

Decorative tile vents, spiral pilasters and wrought-iron window treatments achieve a seamless fusion with the powerful, New-Century look of this modern revival elevation. Interior vistas mix it up with sunlight and fresh breezes through the plan, with walls of glass that extend living spaces to the outdoors. A high beamed ceiling, crafted cabinetry and massive hearth achieve a colonial character that is seamlessly fused with state-of-the art amenities: retreating walls, wide-open rooms, and sleek, do-everything appliances.

Bed: **4**   Bath: **3-1/2**

Width: **67'0"**   Depth: **91'8"**

Level One: **3166** sq ft

Living Area: **3166** sq ft

Exterior Wall:

8" CBS OR 2x6

Foundation: slab

SATER DESIGN PLAN

See price index pages 186-187

REAR VIEW

© THE SATER DESIGN COLLECTION, INC.

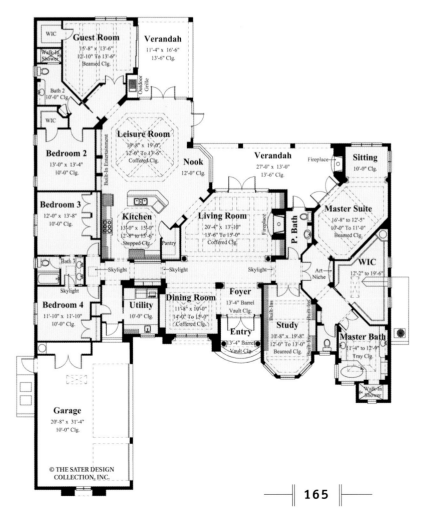

© THE SATER DESIGN COLLECTION, INC.

Spanish | 8066

VILLA

TEODORA

A grand cupola, bay turret and a recessed arch entry adorn this Spanish-inspired home. Inside, rooms are embellished with fine details—built-in cabinetry, fireplaces, art niches and specialty ceilings. The kitchen features an eating bar that connects to the nook and spacious leisure room. Separate verandahs offer intimacy around an outdoor fireplace and a party center around a built-in grille. Three bedrooms plus a guest suite provide quiet spaces for family and friends.

Bed: **5**   Bath: **3-1/2**

Width: **80'0"**   Depth: **104'0"**

Level One: **3993** sq ft

Living Area: **3993** sq ft

Exterior Wall:

8" CBS OR 2x6

Foundation: slab

BEST LIVABILITY DESIGN AWARD

SATER DESIGN PLAN

See price index pages 186-187

www.europeanhouseplans.com

© THE SATER DESIGN COLLECTION, INC.

REAR VIEW

Spanish | 8049

RENAISSANCE

CORSINI

Corbels, columns and carved balusters rooted in a timeless Spanish vocabulary establish a striking street prescence. Inside, the foyer opens to the great room, an outside-in space that brings in breezes and links with nature. A lateral arrangement of the kitchen, loggia, nook and formal dining room eases entertaining. To the right of the plan, the owners' wing opens to the terrace. The upper-level loft overlooks the great room and connects four guest bedrooms.

Bed: **5** Bath: **3-1/2**

Width: **71'0"** Depth: **72'0"**

Level One: **2163** sq ft

Level Two: **1415** sq ft

Living Area: **3578** sq ft

Exterior Wall: **2x6**

Foundation: slab or optional basement

BEST 2-STORY PLAN DESIGN

SATER DESIGN PLAN

See price index pages 186-187

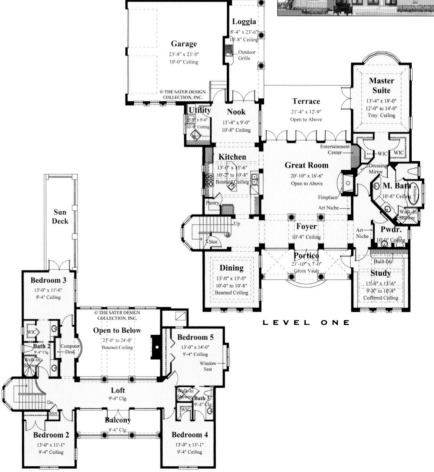

LEVEL ONE

LEVEL TWO

REAR VIEW

© THE SATER DESIGN COLLECTION, INC.

WWW.EUROPEANHOUSEPLANS.COM

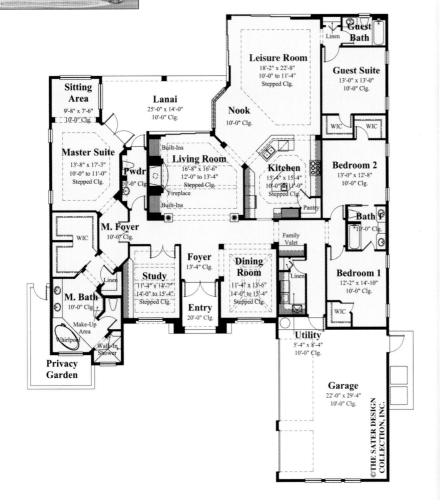

Sitting Area
9'-8" x 7'-6"
10'-0" Clg.

Lanai
25'-0" x 14'-0"
10'-0" Clg.

Nook
10'-0" Clg.

Leisure Room
18'-2" x 22'-8"
10'-0" to 11'-4"
Stepped Clg.

Guest Bath

Linen

Guest Suite
13'-0" x 13'-0"
10'-0" Clg.

Master Suite
13'-8" x 17'-3"
10'-0" to 11'-0"
Stepped Clg.

Built-Ins

Living Room
16'-8" x 16'-6"
12'-0" to 13'-4"
Stepped Clg.

Fireplace

Built-Ins

Pwdr
10'-0" Clg.

Kitchen
15'-4" x 15'-4"
10'-0" x 11'-0"
Stepped Clg.

WIC

WIC

Bedroom 2
13'-0" x 12'-8"
10'-0" Clg.

Pantry

Bath
10'-0" Clg.

M. Foyer
10'-0" Clg.

WIC

Family Valet

Linen

Bedroom 1
12'-2" x 14'-10"
10'-0" Clg.

M. Bath
10'-0" Clg.

Make-Up Area

Whirlpool

Walk-In Shower

Study
11'-4" x 14'-2"
14'-0" to 15'-4"
Stepped Clg.

Foyer
13'-4" Clg.

Dining Room
11'-4" x 13'-6"
14'-0" to 15'-4"
Stepped Clg.

Entry
20'-0" Clg.

Linen

WIC

Privacy Garden

Utility
5'-4" x 8'-4"
10'-0" Clg.

Garage
22'-0" x 29'-4"
10'-0" Clg.

©THE SATER DESIGN COLLECTION, INC.

© THE SATER DESIGN COLLECTION, INC.

Spanish | 8061

ROCOCO REVIVAL

MARTELLI

A sculpted, recessed entry defines the finely detailed Spanish eclectic façade, and a quatrefoil window confirms a Moorish influence. Inside, an open arrangement of the foyer and the formal rooms permits natural light to flow freely through the space. Walls of glass to the rear of the plan open the public and private realms to spectacular views, while nearby, the gourmet kitchen easily serves planned events both inside and out.

Bed: **4**   Bath: **3-1/2**

Width: **68'8"**   Depth: **91'8"**

Level One: **3497** sq ft

Living Area: **3497** sq ft

Exterior Wall:

8" CBS OR 2x6

Foundation: slab

FAMILY-FRIENDLY LIVING DESIGN

SATER DESIGN PLAN

See price index pages 186-187

8070 LEIGHTON

English Old-World elegance balances modern sensibilities to create home plans with a strong sense of history and beauty. Combining the very best of formal design with casual comfort, these English-inspired homes offer unique and exciting opportunities for gracious family living. Rugged exterior textures, stately gables and pediments, arches and plentiful windows create a welcoming ambiance reminiscent of the English countryside. Inside, experience the impact of beautifully detailed staircases, vaulted, beamed and stepped ceilings, and copious views of the open rooms and outdoor living areas.

REAR VIEW

© THE SATER DESIGN COLLECTION, INC.

WWW.EUROPEANHOUSEPLANS.COM

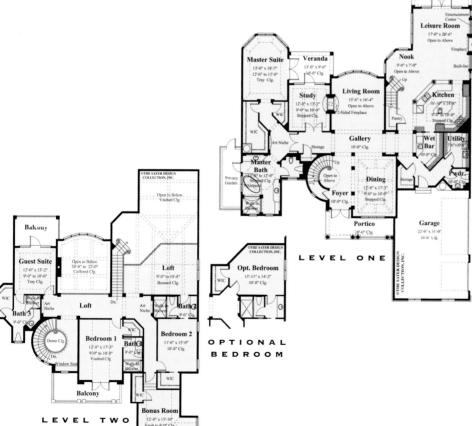

English | 8013
COUNTRY RURAL

COACH HILL

A striking balcony, bay turret and pediment dormers add curb appeal to this English country design. The foyer surrounds a spiral staircase, enhanced with a dome ceiling and clerestory windows. A stepped ceiling and arched columns define the forward formal room, permitting an unobstructed view of the rear property. Plenty of natural light enters the living room through the two-story bow window, which shares a two-sided fireplace with the study.

Bed: **4**   Bath: **4-1/2**

Width: **70'0"**   Depth: **100'0"**

Level One: **3018** sq ft

Level Two: **1646** sq ft

Living Area: **4664** sq ft

Bonus Room: **294** sq ft

Exterior Wall: **2x6**

Foundation: slab or optional basement

SATER DESIGN PLAN

See price index pages 186-187

WWW.EUROPEANHOUSEPLANS.COM © THE SATER DESIGN COLLECTION, INC.

REAR VIEW

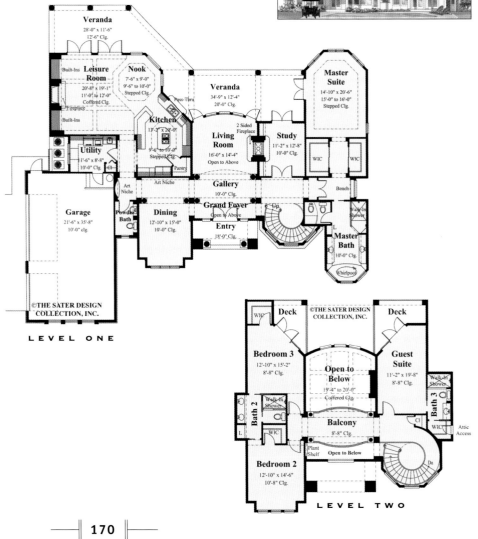

English | 8002
COTSWOLD

CLARISSANT

Two-story bays, a renaissance entry and overlapping gables enhance the presentation of this English-inspired manor. Inside, a gallery links the grand foyer with the formal rooms—a study, formal dining room and a palatial living room that flows outdoors. Built-ins and a fireplace anchor the leisure space that also expands to the veranda. A stunning spiral staircase leads to upper-level sleeping quarters that are connected by a balcony hall overlooking the foyer and living room.

Bed: **4** Bath: **3-1/2**

Width: **85'0"** Depth: **76'8"**

Level One: **2829** sq ft

Level Two: **1127** sq ft

Living Area: **3956** sq ft

Exterior Wall: **2x6**

Foundation: slab or optional basement

SATER DESIGN PLAN

See price index pages 186-187

© THE SATER DESIGN COLLECTION, INC.

REAR VIEW

© THE SATER DESIGN COLLECTION, INC.

LEVEL ONE

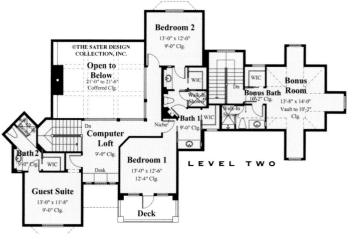

LEVEL TWO

English | 8006
REGENCY

BERKLEY

Pedimented gables, carved balusters and shutters evoke a 19th-century theme, while a wide-open interior emphasizes the benefits of changing seasons. Intentionally informal and cottage-like on the outside, the core of the plan reveals an array of columns, arches and sculpted architectural furnishings. Bay windows punctuate the formal and casual zones, letting in light and the great outdoors. Upstairs, a computer loft overlooks the great room and links three guest bedrooms.

Bed: **4**   Bath: **3-1/2**

Width: **91'0"**   Depth: **52'8"**

Level One: **2219** sq ft

Level Two: **1085** sq ft

Living Area: **3304** sq ft

Bonus Room: **405** sq ft

Exterior Wall: **2x6**

Foundation: slab

SATER DESIGN PLAN

See price index pages 186-187

www.europeanhouseplans.com   © THE SATER DESIGN COLLECTION, INC.

REAR VIEW

English | **8008**

RURAL

NEW ABBEY

Stone and stucco create an idyllic presence with this British-inspired design. Inside, the private and public realms are arranged laterally, achieving a natural flow. Specialty ceilings and arched passages unify the central space—three unique rooms that share an orientation to the rear of the plan, allowing great views. The master retreat features retreating walls to the veranda. The opposing side of the plan harbors the informal zone—the kitchen, an inside/outside leisure room and two guest bedrooms.

Bed: **3**   Bath: **3-1/2**

Width: **106'4"**   Depth: **102'4"**

Level One: **3664** sq ft

Living Area: **3664** sq ft

Exterior Wall: **2x6**

Foundation: slab, optional basement or optional walkout

SUPERB OUTDOOR · LIVING DESIGN

SATER DESIGN PLAN

See price index pages 186-187

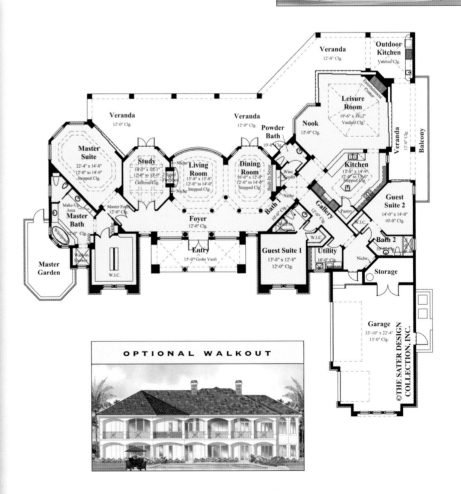

OPTIONAL WALKOUT

© THE SATER DESIGN COLLECTION, INC.

WWW.EUROPEANHOUSEPLANS.COM

REAR VIEW

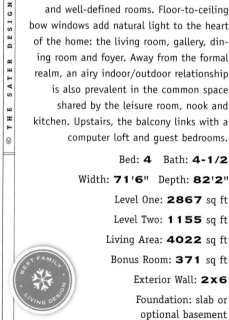

© THE SATER DESIGN COLLECTION, INC.

LEVEL ONE

LEVEL TWO

English | **8012**

REGENCY RURAL

ELISE

This English-inspired façade surrounds a sophisticated interior of wide-open spaces and well-defined rooms. Floor-to-ceiling bow windows add natural light to the heart of the home: the living room, gallery, dining room and foyer. Away from the formal realm, an airy indoor/outdoor relationship is also prevalent in the common space shared by the leisure room, nook and kitchen. Upstairs, the balcony links with a computer loft and guest bedrooms.

Bed: **4** Bath: **4-1/2**

Width: **71'6"** Depth: **82'2"**

Level One: **2867** sq ft

Level Two: **1155** sq ft

Living Area: **4022** sq ft

Bonus Room: **371** sq ft

Exterior Wall: **2x6**

Foundation: slab or optional basement

BEST FAMILY · LIVING DESIGN

SATER DESIGN PLAN

See price index pages 186-187

www.europeanhouseplans.com © THE SATER DESIGN COLLECTION, INC.

REAR VIEW

English | **8016**

REVIVAL

AUBREY

Wrought-iron balustrades and sculpted masonry define a classic elevation that is anchored by a stunning side turret, twin dormers and Doric columns. Arches and columns frame the foyer and gallery, flanked by well-defined formal rooms. At the heart of the home, a spacious leisure room leads to the veranda through French doors. The opposing turret harbors a spiral staircase and a loft that links with the balcony and sleeping quarters.

Bed: **4**   Bath: **3-1/2**

Width: **83'0"**   Depth: **71'8"**

Level One: **2484** sq ft

Level Two: **1127** sq ft

Living Area: **3611** sq ft

Bonus Room: **332** sq ft

Exterior Wall: **2x6**

Foundation: slab or optional basement

BEST 2-STORY PLAN DESIGN

SATER DESIGN PLAN

See price index pages 186-187

© THE SATER DESIGN COLLECTION, INC.

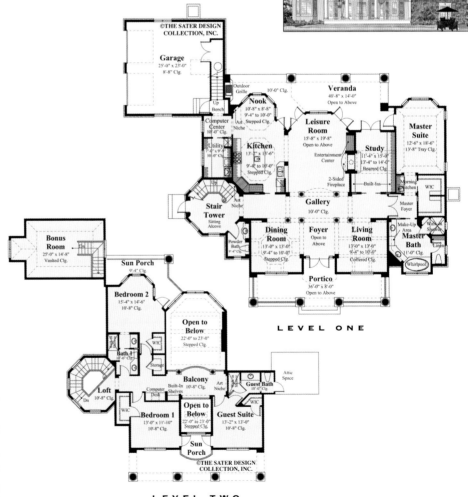

LEVEL ONE

LEVEL TWO

REAR VIEW

© THE SATER DESIGN COLLECTION, INC.

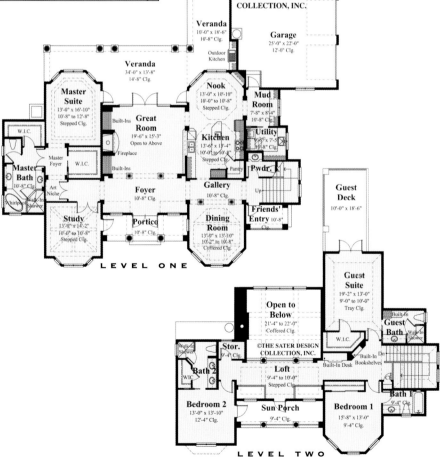

©THE SATER DESIGN COLLECTION, INC.

Veranda
10'-0" x 18'-6"
10'-8" Clg.

Garage
25'-0" x 22'-0"
12'-0" Clg.

Outdoor Kitchen

Veranda
34'-0" x 13'-8"
14'-8" Clg.

Nook
13'-0" x 10'-10"
10'-0" to 10'-8"
Stepped Clg.

Mud Room
7'-8" x 8'-4"
10'-8" Clg.

Master Suite
13'-0" x 16'-10"
10'-8" to 12'-8"
Stepped Clg.

Great Room
19'-6" x 15'-3"
Open to Above

Built-Ins

Kitchen
13'-6" x 13'-4"
10'-0" to 10'-8"
Stepped Clg.

Utility
7'-5"
10'-8" Clg.

Fireplace

W.I.C.

Pantry

Built-Ins

Master Foyer

W.I.C.

Master Bath
10'-8" Clg.

Art Niche

Whirlpool

Walk-In Shower

Foyer
10'-8" Clg.

Gallery
10'-8" Clg.

Pwdr.

Up

Friends' Entry
10'-8" Clg.

Study
13'-0" x 14'-2"
10'-6" to 10'-8"
Stepped Clg.

Portico
10'-8" Clg.

Dining Room
13'-0" x 13'-0"
10'-2" to 10'-8"
Coffered Clg.

LEVEL ONE

Guest Deck
10'-0" x 18'-6"

Guest Suite
19'-2" x 13'-0"
9'-0" to 10'-0"
Tray Clg.

Open to Below
21'-4" to 22'-0"
Coffered Clg.

W.I.C.

Built-In

Guest Bath

Walk-In Shower

Built-In Bookshelves

Built-In Desk

©THE SATER DESIGN COLLECTION, INC.

Walk-In Shower

Stor.
9'-4" Clg.

Bath 2

WIC

Loft
9'-4" to 10'-0"
Stepped Clg.

Dn

Bath 1
9'-4"

Bedroom 2
13'-0" x 13'-10"
12'-4" Clg.

Sun Porch
9'-4" Clg.

Bedroom 1
15'-8" x 13'-0"
9'-4" Clg.

LEVEL TWO

English | **8019**

RURAL

ASCOTT

Vintage lines recall strokes of genius from 19th-century British architecture and marry history with a contempory sanctuary. French doors and bay windows invite fresh air and panoramic views into the private and public realms—which can flex to suit the changing lifestyles of the owners. A friends' entry and side staircase lead to three upper-level guest quarters. Nearby, the loft overlooks the great room and opens to a sun porch.

Bed: **4**   Bath: **4-1/2**

Width: **80'0"**   Depth: **63'9"**

Level One: **2227** sq ft

Level Two: **1278** sq ft

Living Area: **3505** sq ft

Exterior Wall: **2x6**

Foundation: slab or optional basement

FAMILY-FRIENDLY LIVING DESIGN

SATER DESIGN PLAN

See price index pages 186-187

© THE SATER DESIGN COLLECTION, INC.

www.europeanhouseplans.com

© THE SATER DESIGN COLLECTION, INC.

REAR VIEW

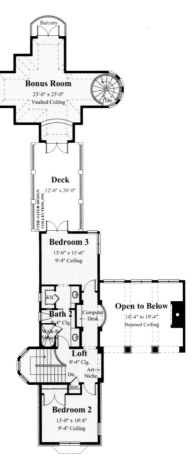

English | **8023**

COUNTRY

EDMONTON

Arcades and rambling terraces glide into airy, contemporary spaces designed for 21st-century living. A massive fireplace anchors the core of the plan—an open arrangement of the foyer and great room that expands to the courtyard through French doors. Gentle breezes infiltrate the casual zone though the loggia, which boasts an outdoor kitchen and connects to the garage where a spiral staircase leads to a versatile bonus room.

Bed: **3**   Bath: **2-1/2**

Width: **60'6"**   Depth: **94'0"**

Level One: **2117** sq ft

Level Two: **652** sq ft

Living Area: **2769** sq ft

Bonus Room: **375** sq ft

Exterior Wall: **2x6**

Foundation: slab or optional basement

SATER DESIGN PLAN

See price index pages 186-187

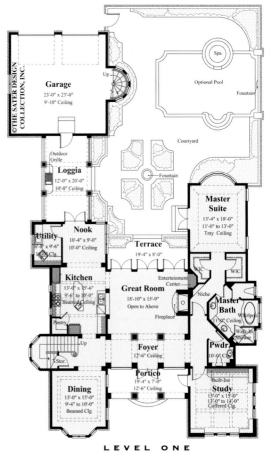

LEVEL ONE

LEVEL TWO

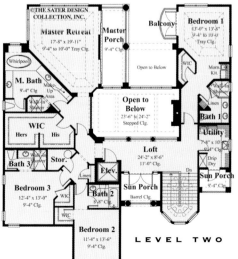

REAR VIEW

© THE SATER DESIGN COLLECTION, INC.   WWW.EUROPEANHOUSEPLANS.COM

© THE SATER DESIGN COLLECTION, INC.

Porch 10'-0" Clg.
Leisure Room 17'-8" x 19'-11" 9'-4" to 10'-0" Stepped Clg.
Entertainment Center
Cabana/Guest Suite 13'-0" x 13'-4" 10'-0" Clg.

Nook 9'-0" x 9'-8" 9'-4" Clg.
Veranda 26'-6" x 10'-7" Open to Above
Outdoor Grille
Guest Bath Walk-In Shower

Kitchen 17'-4" x 13'-8" 9'-4" to 10'-0" Stepped Clg.
Living/Dining Room 21'-11" x 11'-9" Open to Above Two Sided Fireplace
Built-Ins

Pantry
Pwdr.
Library / Study 12'-3" x 15'-0" 9'-4" to 10'-0" Stepped Clg.

Foyer 10'-0" Clg.
Elev.
Stor.
Up
Stor.
Porch 10'-0" Clg.

Garage 29'-0" x 23'-8" 10'-0" Clg.
Entry 10'-0" Clg.

©THE SATER DESIGN COLLECTION, INC.

LEVEL ONE

©THE SATER DESIGN COLLECTION, INC.

Master Retreat 17'-8" x 19'-11" 9'-4" to 10'-0" Tray Clg.
Master Porch 9'-4" Clg.
Balcony
Bedroom 1 13'-0" x 13'-8" 9'-4" to 10'-0" Tray Clg.

Whirlpool
M. Bath 9'-4" Clg.
Make-Up Area
Walk-In Shower
Open to Below
WIC
Morn. Kit.
Walk-In Shower

WIC Hers His
Open to Below 23'-6" to 24'-2" Stepped Clg.
Linen
Bath 1

Bath 3
Stor.
Elev.
Loft 24'-2" x 8'-6" 11'-0" Clg.
Utility 7'-8" x 10' 9'-4" Clg.
Drip Dry

Bedroom 3 12'-4" x 13'-0" 9'-4" Clg.
WIC
Bath 2 8'-8" Clg.
Sun Porch Barrel Clg.
Dn
Sun Porch 9'-4" Clg.
Linen
WIC

Bedroom 2 11'-4" x 13'-6" 9'-4" Clg.

LEVEL TWO

English | **8027**

REGENCY

BELLAMARE

An appealing blend of stone and stucco conveys the charm of the British country-side. Past the foyer, the central living space presents a formal composition designed for planned events and dining, enhanced with a two-sided fireplace shared with the study. To facilitate less formal meals, the common living areas open to a wraparound veranda. An elevator offers an alternative to the spiral staircase that leads to the upper-level bedrooms and loft.

Bed: **5**   Bath: **5-1/2**

Width: **58'0"**   Depth: **65'0"**

Level One: **1996** sq ft

Level Two: **2171** sq ft

Living Area: **4167** sq ft

Exterior Wall: **2x6**

Foundation: slab or optional basement

VIEW ORIENTED · LIVING DESIGN

SATER DESIGN PLAN

See price index pages 186-187

THE SATER DESIGN COLLECTION, INC.

REAR VIEW

English | 8029

REVIVAL

HAMILTON

Freely interpreted revival elements empower a country theme with this neo-English manor. With one-story functionality, this deeply comfortable interior easily adapts to the owner's lifestyle. Formal rooms are defined by columns and specialty ceilings. Nearby, the great room enjoys unrestrained access to the veranda through French doors. An extended-hearth fireplace carries warmth to the kitchen and nook area. Guest bedrooms cluster near the casual zone, while a secluded master suite offers repose for the owners.

Bed: **3**   Bath: **2-1/2**

Width: **62'10"**   Depth: **73'6"**

Level One: **2194** sq ft

Living Area: **2194** sq ft

Exterior Wall: **2x6**

Foundation: slab or optional basement

SATER DESIGN PLAN

See price index pages 186-187

REAR VIEW

© THE SATER DESIGN COLLECTION, INC.

WWW.EUROPEANHOUSEPLANS.COM

LEVEL ONE

LEVEL TWO

© THE SATER DESIGN COLLECTION, INC.

English | 8031

BRITISH VERNACULAR

GULLANE

Rows of windows punctuate a stucco façade, which integrates classic lines with an oceanfront attitude. The spirit throughout the house is formal, yet extends a sense of welcome to guests. Open, public spaces are framed by columns and beamed ceilings, with floor-to-ceiling windows in the living room offering commanding views. Retreating glass walls intergrate the common living space with the loggia. Upstairs, guest bedrooms and the master retreat enjoy repose.

Bed: **5**   Bath: **5-1/2**

Width: **58'0"**   Depth: **65'0"**

Level One: **2164** sq ft

Level Two: **2311** sq ft

Living Area: **4475** sq ft

Exterior Wall: **2x6**

Foundation: slab or optional basement

SATER DESIGN PLAN

See price index pages 186-187

REAR VIEW

English | 8036

GOTHIC

MAITENA

Lancet windows with intersecting Gothic tracery, transoms and side panels establish a stunning street presence, evocative of 18th-century England. Past the foyer, stepped ceilings define the formal rooms. Retreating glass walls open the leisure room to the outside amenities and invite a sense of nature into the casual zone. A walk-in wet bar adjoins the kitchen and provides a servery to the formal dining room. To the right of the plan, the master wing enjoys repose.

Bed: **3** Bath: **4**

Width: **83'10"** Depth: **106'0"**

Level One: **3942** sq ft

Living Area: **3942** sq ft

Exterior Wall: **2x6**

Foundation: slab

SATER DESIGN PLAN

See price index pages 186-187

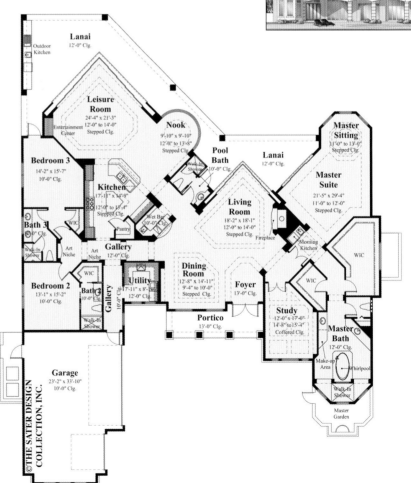

REAR VIEW

© THE SATER DESIGN COLLECTION, INC.

WWW.EUROPEANHOUSEPLANS.COM

©THE SATER DESIGN COLLECTION, INC.

LEVEL ONE

©THE SATER DESIGN COLLECTION, INC.

Deck
26'-0" x 15'-10"

Bedroom 1
13'-0" x 14'-6"
9'-4" to 10'-4"
Tray Clg.

Bedroom 2
12'-2" x 14'-4"
10'-0" Clg.

Bath 2
10'-0" Clg.

WIC

Loft
10'-0" Clg.

Desk   Niche

Dn.

Bonus Bath

Bonus Room
16'-6" x 21'-6"
Vaulted to 9'-8" Clg.

LEVEL TWO

LAURETTE — ELEVATION B
*Call for plan details

Floor plan labels (Level One)

Lanai 26'-0" x 15'-10" 10'-0" Clg.

Master Suite 13'-2" x 21'-2" 12'-0" to 13'-0" Stepped Clg.

Great Room 21'-3" x 17'-8" Vaulted w/ Beamed Clg.

Nook 9'-0" x 10'-0" Stepped Clg.

Bath 1

Dining Room 11'-10" x 12'-8" 9'-0" to 10'-0" Coffered Clg.

Kitchen 13'-0" x 3'-9" 9'-0" to 9'-6" Stepped Clg.

Fireplace

Entertainment Center

Built-In Shelves

WIC   WIC   Walk-in Shower

Foyer 18'-8" to 19'-8" Stepped Clg.

Gallery 10'-0" Clg.

Utility 6'-8" x 12'-0" 10'-0" Clg.

Master Bath 12'-0" Clg.

Study 11'-0" x 15'-4" 16'-4" to 17'-4" Beamed Clg.

Pwdr. 10'-0" Clg.

Storage

Up

Whirlpool

Entry 18'-8" Clg.

Garage 21'-0" x 25'-4" 10'-0" Clg.

$\mathscr{E}$nglish | 8038

TUDOR

CHADWICK — ELEVATION A

Vintage lines honor the rural English provenance of this rustic manor. Inside, floor-to-
ceiling windows and French doors bring in
light and extend the living spaces outward.
Ceiling treatments define the open rooms
of the central interior. Nearby, a bay window harbors the nook and brings in views
shared with the kitchen. The wrapping
lanai is accessible from the great room,
formal dining room and nook. Upstairs, two
guest bedrooms share a sun deck.

Bed: **3**   Bath: **3-1/2**

Width: **72'0"**   Depth: **68'3"**

Level One: **2250** sq ft

Level Two: **663** sq ft

Living Area: **2913** sq ft

Bonus Room: **351** sq ft

Exterior Wall: **2x6**

Foundation: slab

FAMILY-FRIENDLY LIVING DESIGN

SATER DESIGN PLAN

See price index pages 186-187

REAR VIEW

www.europeanhouseplans.com   © THE SATER DESIGN COLLECTION, INC.

English | **8041**

REVIVAL

WELLINGTON

Evocative of early revival homes, this English manor melds a sophisticated brick-and-stucco façade with the kind of livable amenities that endear a home to its owners. A gallery foyer grants vistas that extend to the rear veranda—via an airy living/dining room with a beamed ceiling. French doors bordering the master and formal wings integrate the interior with the outdoors, while retreating glass doors expand the common living space to the veranda.

Bed: **3**   Bath: **2** Full & **2** Half

Width: **84'0"**   Depth: **92'0"**

Level One: **3353** sq ft

Living Area: **3353** sq ft

Exterior Wall: **2x6**

Foundation: slab

SATER DESIGN PLAN

See price index pages 186-187

REAR VIEW

© THE SATER DESIGN COLLECTION, INC.

WWW.EUROPEANHOUSEPLANS.COM

Veranda
20'-0" x 19'-7"
Flat Clg.

Outdoor Grille

Guest Bath

Guest Suite
11'-8" x 16'-0"
Flat Clg.

Storage

WIC

Leisure Room
18'-8" x 15'-9"
Stepped Clg.

Entertainment Center

Game Room
12'-8" x 13'-11"
Stepped Clg.

Sitting Area
10'-0" x 7'-11"
Flat Clg.

Veranda
33'-11" x 14'-0"
Flat Clg.

Nook
7'-0" x 9'-8"
Flat Clg.

Master Suite
16'-10" x 16'-9"
Stepped Clg.

Living Room
18'-9" x 13'-10"
Coffered Clg.

Fireplace

Kitchen
Stepped Clg.

Pantry

Bedroom 2
12'-2" x 13'-0"
Flat Clg.

Pwdr.

Built-Ins

Gallery

Window Seat

Bath 1

Walk-In Shower

WIC

Art Niche

Master Bath
Flat Clg.

Make-up Area

Whirlpool

Walk-In Shower

WIC

Study
13'-0" x 14'-10"
Beamed Clg.

Built-Ins

Foyer

Dining Room
12'-0" x 14'-2"
Stepped Clg.

Utility

Bedroom 1
12'-2" x 12'-0"
Flat Clg.

Portico
36'-0" x 7'-0"

Storage

Garage
21'-0" x 40'-6"
Flat Clg.

©THE SATER DESIGN COLLECTION, INC.

Leisure Room
19'-2" x 15'-9"
Stepped Clg.

Entertainment Center

Optional Bedroom 3
12'-4" x 13'-11"
Flat Clg.

©THE SATER DESIGN COLLECTION, INC.

OPTIONAL 3RD BEDROOM

© THE SATER DESIGN COLLECTION, INC.

English | **8045**

CLASSIC REVIVAL

DEMETRI

Stately Corinthian columns and a trio of pediments set off this revival façade. The interior progresses from the foyer and formal rooms to a central living space that flexes to facilitate planned events as well as cozy family gatherings. As the plan unfolds to the right, halls lead separately to the airy, indoor/outdoor casual zone and to the guest bedrooms. Secluded to the other side of the home is the generous master retreat.

Bed: **4**   Bath: **3-1/2**

Width: **80'0"**   Depth: **108'0"**

Level One: **3764** sq ft

Living Area: **3764** sq ft

Exterior Wall: **2x6**

Foundation: slab or optional basement

BEST 1-STORY PLAN DESIGN

SATER DESIGN PLAN

See price index pages 186-187

www.europeanhouseplans.com   © THE SATER DESIGN COLLECTION, INC.

REAR VIEW

English | **8050**

NEO-CLASSIC

KENDRICK

A triplet of paneled doors leads through the foyer to a spectacular great room with unimpeded views of the rear property. Art niches and a massive hearth define one wall of the great room, and contradict an opposing series of flat soffits that open the space to the kitchen. To the right of the plan, the master wing sports a luxe bath. Upstairs, a balcony loft links four bedrooms and leads to the front deck.

Bed: **5**   Bath: **3-1/2**

Width: **71'0"**   Depth: **72'0"**

Level One: **2163** sq ft

Level Two: **1415** sq ft

Living Area: **3578** sq ft

Exterior Wall: **2x6**

Foundation: slab

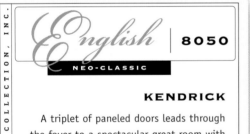

SATER DESIGN PLAN

See price index pages 186-187

LEVEL ONE

LEVEL TWO

REAR VIEW

© THE SATER DESIGN COLLECTION, INC.

WWW.EUROPEANHOUSEPLANS.COM

LEVEL TWO

Balcony
10'-12" x 9'-4"

Grand Room
Beamed Clg.
Open to Below

Bedroom 2
10'-11" x 13'-4"
10'-0" Clg.

©THE SATER DESIGN COLLECTION, INC.

Balcony
10'-7" x 14'-4"

Bedroom 3
15'-0" x 11'-6"
10'-0" Clg.

Bath 2
10'-0" Clg.

Bath 3

Bedroom 4
11'-6" x 16'-8"
10'-0" Clg.

Balcony

LEVEL ONE

Loggia
26'-10" x 11'-8"
Open to Above

Loggia
15'-6" x 10'-0"
10'-0" Clg.

Master Suite
14'-8" x 22'-4"
12'-0" to 14'-0"
Stepped Clg.

Grand Room
19'-0" x 19'-5"
Open to Above

Dining Room
10'-6" x 13'-4"
10'-0" Clg.

M. Bath
12'-0" to 14'-0"
Stepped Clg.

Whirlpool

WIC

Pwdr.
9'-4" Clg.

Foyer

Utility

Walk-In Shower

Linen

Study
14'-4" x 15'-0"
12'-0" to 13'-0"
Stepped Clg.

Loggia
10'-0" Clg.

Desk

Kitchen
13'-8" x 15'-4"
10'-0" Clg.

Nook
10'-0" Clg.

Pantry

Fountain

Spa

Optional Pool

Courtyard

Loggia
16'-8" Clg.

Leisure Room
18'-6" x 17'-10"
10'-0" to 14'-6"
Stepped Clg.

Garage
11'-6" x 16'-10"
10'-0" Clg.

Fireplace

Built-In Entertainment

Loggia
10'-0" Clg.

Outdoor Kitchen

WIC

Guest Suite
14'-4" x 13'-5"
10'-0" Clg.

Pool Bath

Portico
14'-8" x 14'-4"
Groin Vault

Garage
22'-4" x 25'-6"
10'-0" Clg.

©THE SATER DESIGN COLLECTION, INC.

English | **8047**

REVIVAL

GARNETT

Varied rooflines and gables command a powerful street presence yet conceal an enchanting courtyard. Beyond a breezy portico and detached guest suite, the courtyard leads to the formal entry. Past the foyer, the grand room features two-story bay windows that extend the footprint of the home. Centrally located, the kitchen easily serves the formal and informal rooms. Secluded from the public realm is the master retreat. Upstairs, guest rooms enjoy balcony access.

Bed: **5**   Bath: **4-1/2**

Width: **80'0"**   Depth: **96'6"**

Level One: **2852** sq ft

Level Two: **969** sq ft

Bonus Room: **330** sq ft

Living Area: **4151** sq ft

Exterior Wall: **2x6**

Foundation: slab

BEST 2-STORY PLAN DESIGN

SATER DESIGN PLAN

See price index pages 186-187

PLAN NAME	PLAN #	PRINT LICENSE	ELECTRONIC LICENSE	SQ. FT.	PAGE	STYLE
Casina Rossa	8071	$1,315	$2,410	2,191	115	Tuscan
Kinsley	8030	$1,315	$2,410	2,191	150	French
Mercato	8028	$1,315	$2,410	2,191	159	Spanish
Hamilton	8029	$1,316	$2,413	2,194	178	English
Bartolini	8022	$1,642	$3,010	2,736	131	Italian
Gabriel	8024	$1,642	$3,010	2,736	148	French
Edmonton	8023	$1,661	$3,046	2,769	176	English
Chadwick A or B	8038	$1,748	$3,204	2,913	181	English
Medoro	8039	$1,748	$3,204	2,913	140	French
Raphaello	8037	$1,748	$3,204	2,913	134	Italian
Ferretti*	6786	$1,819	$3,334	3,031	108	Tuscan
Porta Rossa	8058	$1,900	$3,483	3,166	164	Spanish
Simone	8059	$1,939	$3,554	3,231	123	Tuscan
Le Marescott	8060	$1,948	$3,571	3,246	152	French
Caprina	8052	$1,963	$3,598	3,271	163	Spanish
Christabel	8053	$1,963	$3,598	3,271	156	French
Channing	8005	$1,978	$3,627	3,297	141	French
Berkley	8006	$1,982	$3,634	3,304	171	English
Chadbryne	8004	$1,982	$3,634	3,304	119	Tuscan
Bellini	8042	$2,011	$3,686	3,351	135	Italian
Brittany	8040	$2,012	$3,688	3,353	153	French
Wellington	8041	$2,012	$3,688	3,353	182	English
Salcito	6787	$2,075	$3,804	3,458	117	Tuscan
Martelli	8061	$2,098	$3,847	3,497	167	Spanish
Santa Trinita	8063	$2,098	$3,847	3,497	124	Tuscan
New Brunswick	8021	$2,101	$3,851	3,501	147	French
Vienna	8020	$2,101	$3,851	3,501	121	Tuscan
Ascott	8019	$2,103	$3,856	3,505	175	English
Corsini	8049	$2,147	$3,936	3,578	166	Spanish
Kendrick	8050	$2,147	$3,936	3,578	184	English
Solaine	8051	$2,147	$3,936	3,578	155	French
Bellamy	8018	$2,166	$3,971	3,610	146	French
Aubrey	8016	$2,167	$3,972	3,611	174	English
Les Tourelles	8017	$2,168	$3,974	3,613	145	French
Baxter	8009	$2,191	$4,017	3,652	142	French
Della Porta	8007	$2,192	$4,019	3,654	128	Italian
New Abbey	8008	$2,198	$4,030	3,664	172	English
Salina	8043	$2,246	$4,117	3,743	132	Italian
Margherita	8075	$3,340	$5,845	3,752	118	Tuscan
Demetri	8045	$3,011	$5,270	3,764	183	English

PLAN NAME	PLAN #	PRINT LICENSE	ELECTRONIC LICENSE	SQ. FT.	PAGE	STYLE
Beauchamp	8044	$3,032	$5,306	3,790	154	French
Laparelli	8035	$3,154	$5,519	3,942	133	Italian
Maitena	8036	$3,154	$5,519	3,942	180	English
Winthrop*	8034	$3,163	$5,536	3,954	76	French
Alessandra	8003	$3,165	$5,538	3,956	127	Italian
Clarissant	8002	$3,157	$5,524	3,956	170	English
Royal Country Down	8001	$3,165	$5,538	3,956	139	French
Teodora	8066	$3,194	$5,590	3,993	165	Spanish
La Riviere	8011	$3,204	$5,607	4,005	143	French
Capucina	8010	$3,209	$5,615	4,011	129	Italian
Elise	8012	$3,218	$5,631	4,022	173	English
La Serena*	8076	$3,239	$5,669	4,049	82	Italian
La Reina*	8046	$3,321	$5,811	4,151	60	Italian
Garnett	8047	$3,321	$5,811	4,151	185	English
Monte Rosa	8077	$3,323	$5,816	4,154	120	Tuscan
Vasari*	8025	$3,328	$5,824	4,160	100	Italian
Bellamare	8027	$3,334	$5,834	4,167	177	English
Saint-Germain	8026	$3,334	$5,834	4,167	149	French
Mezzina	8073	$3,340	$5,845	4,175	136	Italian
Palazzo Ripoli	8074	$3,413	$5,972	4,266	161	Spanish
San Filippo*	8055	$3,513	$6,147	4,391	52	Italian
Argentellas	8056	$3,518	$6,157	4,398	157	French
Massimo	8057	$3,518	$6,157	4,398	122	Tuscan
Isabella	8033	$3,572	$6,251	4,465	130	Italian
Stonehaven	8032	$3,572	$6,251	4,465	151	French
Gullane	8031	$3,580	$6,265	4,475	179	English
Martinique*	6932	$3,594	$6,289	4,492	36	Spanish
Tre Mori	8078	$3,645	$6,378	4,556	160	Spanish
Burke House	8015	$3,717	$6,504	4,646	144	French
Coach Hill	8013	$3,731	$6,530	4,664	169	English
Di Mora*	6954	$3,731	$6,530	4,664	46	Italian
San Lorenzo	8014	$3,731	$6,530	4,664	162	Spanish
Flagstone Ridge	6765	Call for pricing		4,809	137	Italian
Trevi	8065	Call for pricing		4,837	125	Tuscan
Leighton*	8070	Call for pricing		4,958	88	English
Andros Island*	6927	Call for pricing		5,169	42	English
Sancho*	6947	Call for pricing		5,335	94	Spanish
Domenico	8069	Call for pricing		6,126	116	Tuscan
Cordillera*	6953	Call for pricing		6,527	26	Spanish
Villa Sabina*	8068	Call for pricing		6,315	66	Tuscan

Plans in print

WHAT'S IN A SET OF PLANS?

EACH SET OF PLANS IS A COLLECTION OF DRAWINGS THAT REFLECT IMPORTANT STRUCTURAL COMPONENTS, SHOWING HOW YOUR HOME IS TO BE BUILT. MOST OF OUR PLAN PACKAGES INCLUDE THE FOLLOWING:

COVER SHEET/INDEX & SITE PLAN —
An Artist's Rendering of the exterior of the house shows you approximately how the house will look when built. The Index is a list of the sheets included and page numbers for easy reference. The Site Plan is a scaled footprint of the house to help determine the home placement on a building site.

WALL SECTION/NOTES — This sheet shows section cuts of the exterior wall from the roof down through the foundation. These wall sections specify the home's construction and building materials, and whether the design is single- or multi-story, slab, crawlspace or basement, and concrete block or wood-frame walls. Roofing materials, insulation, floor framing, wall finishes and elevation heights are all shown and referenced.

TYPICAL DETAILS AND NOTES — Architectural and structural elements are detailed for construction purposes. Window and door components, railings and balusters, wood stairs and headers, interior walls and partitions, concrete steps and footings (if applicable) are some of the items detailed extensively. General architectural notes spell out minimum specifications as intended for a Sater-designed home. In addition to your local code requirements and builder's expertise, all facets of the home-building process are addressed.

PLUMBING AND FOUNDATION PLAN —
This sheet gives the foundation layout, fully dimensioned and noted. Foundation references to footings, pads, support walls and plumbing fixture locations are shown. If the plan features a basement, additional columns/walls may be shown accordingly and a floor framing layout may be incorporated into this plan or shown on a separate sheet.

DETAILED FLOOR PLAN — This plan and/or plans indicate the layout of each floor of the house. The home's exterior footprint, openings and interior rooms are carefully dimensioned. Important features such as built-ins, appliances and niches are noted; all doors and windows are identified and specific areas are keyed for section details found on other sheets. Larger homes may have floor plans broken into separate dimension and call-out plans. Detailed door and window schedules and a square-footage breakdown of the house can also generally be found on the floor plan sheet.

REFLECTED CEILING PLAN — One of a Sater Home's most distinguishable features is its highly detailed ceiling treatments. In order to ensure successful implementation, this plan indicates ceiling heights and treatments, as well as referencing details that illustrate profiles and finishes of the appropriate condition. Arches and soffits are also called out to make clear the original design intent.

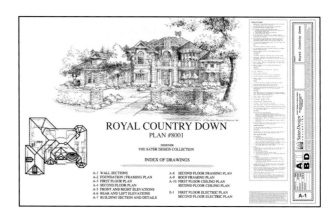

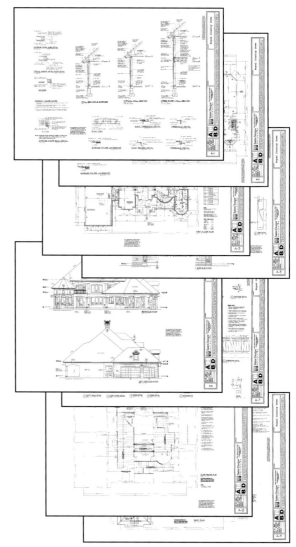

FLOOR FRAMING PLANS — The floor framing plans provide structural information such as joist size, spacing and direction, floor heights and stair openings. Any home with a basement or crawlspace will have a first-floor framing plan and all multi-story homes will have upper-floor framing plans as well.

ROOF PLAN — Overall layout and necessary details for roof design are provided. If trusses are used, we suggest using a local truss manufacturer to design trusses to comply with local codes and regulations.

EXTERIOR ELEVATIONS — Included are front, rear, left side and right side of the house. Exterior materials, details and heights are also given.

CROSS SECTION & DETAILS — Important changes in floor, ceiling and roof heights or the relationship of one level to another are illustrated. Interior elements of certain rooms and areas, such as columns, arches, headers and soffits, are also discernable and easier to visualize in a cross-section. Also shown, when applicable, are exterior details such as railing and banding.

INTERIOR ELEVATIONS — These plans show the specific details and design of kitchens, bathrooms, utility rooms, fireplaces, bookcases, built-in units and other special interior features, depending on the nature and complexity of the home.

ELECTRICAL/LIGHTING PLAN — Because of the detail of Sater-design plans, the Electrical/ Lighting layout is shown on a separate sheet. Our electrical plan is designed to enhance functionality and highlight the unique architectural features of each home.

MATERIALS LIST — To ensure you have every resource possible to assist you in the pricing and construction of your Sater Home, we include free of charge a detailed Materials List with the purchase of every Sater plan.

sater reserve plans — To assist
clients purchasing larger homes, we include all of the above items in Sater Reserve Plans. In addition, we include PLUMBING and ELECTRICAL RISER PLAN information sheets. These items can be purchased separately with all other plans, but come as an added value with your Sater Reserve Plan.

electronic plans

All of the above materials shown for Print Plans are supplied on disk in an Electronic Format that makes for easier revisions.

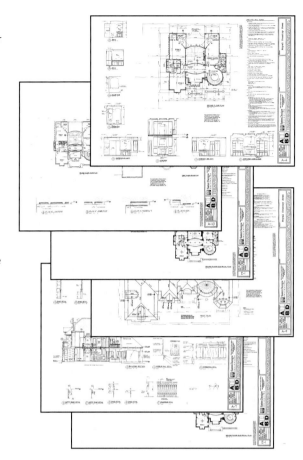

MATERIALS LIST

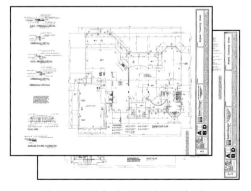

PLUMBING & ELECTRICAL RISER PLANS

Before you order

PLEASE READ THE FOLLOWING HELPFUL INFORMATION

QUICK TURNAROUND
Because you are placing your order directly, we can ship plans to you quickly. If your order is placed before noon EST, we can usually have your plans to you the next business day. Some restrictions may apply. We cannot ship to a post office box; please provide a physical street address.

OUR EXCHANGE POLICY
Since our house plans are printed especially for you at the time you place your order, we cannot accept any returns. If, for some reason, you find that the plan that you purchased does not meet your needs, then you may exchange that plan for another plan in our collection. We allow you sixty days from the time of purchase to make an exchange. At the time of the exchange, you will be charged a processing fee of 20% of the total amount of the original order plus the difference in price between the plans (if applicable) and the cost to ship the new plans to you. All returned sets must be approved and authorization given before the exchange can take place. Please call our customer service department with any questions.

LOCAL BUILDING CODES AND ZONING REQUIREMENTS
Our plans are designed to meet or exceed the International Residential Code. Because of the great differences in geography and climate, each state, county and municipality has its own building codes and zoning requirements. Your plan may need to be modified to comply with local requirements regarding snow loads, energy codes, soil and seismic conditions and a wide range of other matters. Prior to using plans ordered from us, we strongly advise that you consult a local building official.

ARCHITECTURAL AND/OR ENGINEERING REVIEW
Some cities and states are now requiring that a licensed architect or engineer review and approve any set of building documents prior to permitting. This is due to concerns over code compliance, zoning, safety, structural integrity and other factors. Often, an engineer/architect may be required to create accompanying structural drawings in order to obtain permitting. Prior to applying for a building permit or the start of actual construction, we strongly advise that you consult your local building official who can tell you if such a review is required.

DISCLAIMER
We have put substantial care and effort into the creation of our house plans. We authorize the use of our plans on the express condition that you strictly comply with all local building codes, zoning requirements and other applicable laws, regulations and ordinances. However, because we cannot provide on-site consultation, supervision or control over actual construction, and because of the great variance in local building requirements, building practices and soil, seismic, weather and other conditions, WE CANNOT MAKE ANY WARRANTY, EXPRESS OR IMPLIED, WITH RESPECT TO THE CONTENT OR USE OF OUR PLANS, INCLUDING BUT NOT LIMITED TO ANY WARRANTY OF MARKETABILITY OR OF FITNESS FOR A PARTICULAR PURPOSE. Please Note: Floor plans in this book are not construction documents and are subject to change. Renderings are artist's concept only.

HOW MANY SETS OF PRINTS WILL YOU NEED?
For the purposes of obtaining bids, usually one set of plans for each sub-contractor is needed. For permitting purposes, usually three to four sets are required, but check with your local building department. Additional sets may be required if your home is in a planned development and has an architectural review process. Because additional sets are less expensive, make sure you order enough to satisfy all of your requirements, or obtain a reproducible format for making copies locally as needed.

MAKING REVISIONS
Sometimes, changes are needed to a plan. In that case, we offer erasable vellums so minor changes can be made directly to the plans; or, to make more extensive changes, an electronic (CAD) file may be necessary. Vellums or electronic (CAD) files are the only formats that can be reproduced. It is illegal to make copies from prints.

IGNORING COPYRIGHT LAWS CAN BE A

$150,000 mistake!

Recent changes in Federal Copyright Laws allow for statutory penalties of up to $150,000 per incident for copyright infringement involving any of the copyrighted plans found in this publication. The law can be confusing. So, for your own protection, take the time to understand what you cannot do when it comes to home plans.

WHAT YOU CAN'T DO:

- YOU CANNOT BUILD A HOME WITHOUT BUYING A LICENSE.

- YOU CANNOT DUPLICATE HOME PLANS WITHOUT PERMISSION.

- YOU CANNOT COPY ANY PART OF A HOME PLAN TO CREATE ANOTHER.

- YOU MUST OBTAIN A SEPARATE LICENSE EACH TIME YOU BUILD A HOME.

What is a license?

AND OTHER CONSIDERATIONS IN
ORDERING A SATER DESIGN PLAN

PRINT LICENSE	ELECTRONIC LICENSE	HOW TO ORDER
This License is issued in the form of either six sets of Plan Prints or as a single Vellum set. Licensee is entitled to build one home.	This License is issued in the form of an Electronic (CAD) File for the customization and construction of one home.	**ORDER BY PHONE** **1-800-718-7526** **ORDER ONLINE** **www.europeanhouseplans.com** SATER DESIGN COLLECTION 25241 Elementary Way, Suite 201 Bonita Springs, FL 34135

WHAT SETS A SATER PLAN APART?

There are a number of differences you will find in a Sater Design Collection plan versus other home plans on the market. The main reason customers select a Sater Design Plan is for its unique character and original design. In order to ensure the successful implementation of these features, we create highly detailed construction drawings that illustrate each essential element relevant to the Plan. Our Plans are the ultimate guide to building the home of your dreams. Some of the features that you will find in Sater Plans, but not in other plans, are listed below:

	SATER	OTHERS
Extensive Interior Elevations Interior-design quality drawings, showing highly detailed elevations of architectural built-ins and cabinetry	YES	NO
Detailed Materials List To assist the owner/builder with estimating building costs (Offered at no additional charge)	YES	NO
Reflected Ceiling Plans With detailed sections of the numerous ceiling and soffit designs	YES	NO
Separate Electrical/Lighting Plans Carefully designed lighting plans that contemplate your family's use and enjoyment	YES	NO
Detailed Plumbing Plans, Electrical Riser Diagram and Sanitary Riser Schematic (Offered at no additional charge with Sater Reserve Plans)	YES	NO
Unparalleled Customer Support Our dedicated staff is committed to helping you in the decision process	YES	NO

PLAN CUSTOMIZATION SERVICES

When alterations are required to suit your needs, Sater Design Collection also offers an in-house modification service. Call 1-800-718-7526 and speak to a sales representative about your modification needs. A $50 nonrefundable consultation fee will be required before your request can be submitted for review. Many clients consider this option simply to maintain the integrity of the Sater Design, while others find it to be a viable and affordable alternative to a full custom design.

ADDITIONAL ITEMS

15x22 Color Rendering Front Perspective* $195.00

Additional Plan Prints *(per set)* $65.00

Full Reverse Plans* . . . . *special order*

Call for availability and/or pricing.

POSTAGE AND HANDLING

Overnight $54.00

2nd Day $43.00

Ground $33.00

Saturday $74.00

International deliveries: Please call for a quote.

**MEDITERRANEAN
LUXURY HOME PLAN BOOK**

DAN SATER'S MEDITERRANEAN HOME PLANS

65 Mediterranean-style floor plans

In this unmatched portfolio of more than 65 unique home plans you will experience Mediterranean design in a new realm — one that delights, challenges and encourages the imagination. Superb architectural detail infuse sun-baked courtyards and loggias, while open floor plans stretch the boundaries of traditional Mediterranean style.

2,700 to over 8,000 sq ft

$14.95   *192 full-color pages*

**COTTAGES & VILLAS
COASTAL HOME PLAN BOOK**

DAN SATER'S COTTAGES & VILLAS

80 elegant cottage and waterfront home plans

A photo tour of 8 stunning coastal homes previews a portfolio of 80 beautifully rendered and charming clapboard cottages and grand Mediterranean villas. These highly versatile designs are big on open porches and courtyards, while balancing function with style, and bring to mind a relaxed attitude that can only come with view-oriented living.

1,200 to over 4,300 sq ft

$14.95   *224 full-color pages*

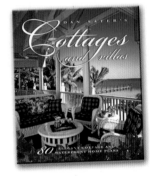

**DAN SATER'S LUXURY
HOME PLAN BOOK**

DAN SATER'S LUXURY HOME PLANS

Over 100 view-oriented estate homes

Here is a colorful and richly textured collection of more than 100 exquisite floor plans. This stunning display of unique Sater homes features more than 220 pages of exciting interior and exterior photography, with unique design ideas for the most gracious living. Whether you're seeking plans for a 6,000-square-foot estate or a 3,000-square-foot villa, you can find them in this truly inspirational portfolio of Dan's best luxury homes.

2,700 to over 8,000 sq ft

$16.95   *256 full-color pages*